The Culinary Institute of America

GRIL

ALSO BY THE CULINARY INSTITUTE OF AMERICA

The Culinary Institute of America's Gourmet Meals in Minutes

Book of Soups • Breakfasts & Brunches

LING

MORE THAN 175 NEW RECIPES FROM THE WORLD'S PREMIER CULINARY COLLEGE

Photography by Ben Fink

LEBHAR-FRIEDMAN BOOKS

NEW YORK ▸ CHICAGO ▸ LOS ANGELES ▸ LONDON ▸ PARIS ▸ TOKYO

THE CULINARY INSTITUTE OF AMERICA

President	Dr. Tim Ryan
Vice-President, Continuing Education	Mark Erickson
Director of Intellectual Property	Nathalie Fischer
Managing Editor	Kate McBride
Editorial Project Manager	Mary Donovan
Editorial Assistant	Margaret Otterstrom
Recipe Testers	Veronica Arcoraci, Alexis Jette-Borggaard, Lisa Lahey, Danny Trotter

The Culinary Institute of America would like to thank chefs Olivier Andreini, Marc Haymon, Bruce Mattel, and John Reilly for their skilled execution and presentation of the recipes and methods for the photographs.

Special thanks to Warren Cutlery in Rhinebeck, New York, and to Weber and Viking for providing some of the items used in the photography.

LEBHAR-FRIEDMAN BOOKS

A company of Lebhar-Friedman, Inc., 425 Park Avenue, New York, New York 10022

LIBRARY OF CONGRESS CATALOGING-IN-PUBLICATION DATA

Cataloging-in-publication data for this title is on file with the Library of Congress.

ISBN 0-86730-905-9 | 978-0-86730-905-8

Manufactured in Singapore on acid-free paper

CONTENTS

MISE EN PLACE FOR GRILLING

GREAT GRILLING DEPENDS upon three basic elements: wonderful food, the right equipment, and good technique. Everyone knows that the best raw materials are at the heart of all good cooking. The recipes throughout this book give you an opportunity to explore familiar and unfamiliar foods on the grill. In this chapter, we concentrate on technique and equipment for getting the most from your grill.

Direct and Indirect Grilling

Controlling the temperature of the grill as foods cook is one of the challenges facing the outdoor chef. Using direct or indirect grilling techniques, or a combination of the two, gives you the flexibility to prepare almost any food on the grill, even large cuts of meat or delicate fruits.

Direct-heat grilling means that foods are placed directly over a lively flame or bed of coals, where the heat is highest and foods cook quickly. This is perfect for small portions like thin steaks or chicken breasts. Depending upon the foods you are cooking, you may need to create a single even layer of coals beneath the entire cooking surface for a charcoal grill.

Indirect-heat grilling means that foods are placed on part of the grill close to but not directly over the heat source. The heat is less intense there, so foods that take longer to cook (such as spareribs) or that might scorch before they finish cooking (pizza or vegetables) can finish cooking without turning black. Techniques for setting up both gas and charcoal grills for direct and indirect heating are described in greater detail in the sections that follow.

Grill and BBQ Tools

A gleaming set of long-handled grilling tools makes grilling easier and safer. There are a number of accessories you can find, and more are being developed all the time.

Grill brushes have wire bristles. Some also have a metal blade to scrape the grill rack. If you don't have a brush handy, you can use a crumpled piece of foil to scour the rack before you begin grilling.

Brushes and mops are used to apply glazes, marinades, and sauces. A long handle keeps your hands and arms out of the heat when grilling over direct heat. You can use regular pastry brushes with shorter handles for delicate foods that are cooked over indirect heat for better control of the brush and less chance of tearing the food you are grilling. Avoid nylon or other materials that might melt. Be sure to clean these tools completely after you use them. It is easy for marinades and sauces to stick to the bristles. Replace these tools as often as necessary.

Spatulas and tongs are indispensable for turning foods and taking them from the grill. Be sure that spatulas are wide enough and long enough to handle the food you are cooking. Delicate foods or small items may call for a narrower or thinner spatula. Bigger items demand heavy-duty tools that won't bend under the weight of the food. To make turning foods easier, try using two spatulas for better control.

Skewers may be bamboo, wood, or metal. Soak bamboo or wooden skewers in cool water so they won't ignite as you grill. Metal skewers don't need any special treatment, but be careful not to touch them when they are still hot from the grill.

Hand racks can hold delicate foods like fish. Some racks have hinges and clamps so that you can close them around the food. If you don't have a hand rack, you can use two cooling racks instead. Wear oven mitts and hold the racks together, trapping the food between them, when you need to turn the food over.

Grill pans and cast-iron skillets or griddles give you greater flexibility when you grill. You can stir-fry foods in a grill wok. Cast-iron skillets or griddles (the same ones you

Grill brush

Grill mop

Large tongs
with teeth for
gripping large
pieces of meat

Various-sized pastry brushes

Carving knife

VIKING

Large carving fork

VIKING

Hand rack

Various sized
offset spatulas

Smaller
carving forks

Small and large
locking tongs

use on your stove or ones made specifically for the grill) let you prepare dishes like pancakes or eggs (see Buckwheat Flapjacks on page 176 or Hoe Cakes on page 151 for examples of this equipment).

Thermometers to check the food's doneness are important to have on hand. You can use single-use thermometers or an instant-read or infrared thermometer to check foods. Insert the thermometer halfway into the food at its thickest part, away from bones if there are any.

A carving knife and fork are essential to have for carving larger pieces of grilled meat. Be sure to move the meat to a cutting board and let it rest before carving it into individual portions.

30" wide Viking gas grill

Types of Grills

A good grill is one that will stand up to years of use, cooks foods evenly, and is easy to clean and maintain. Look for solid construction, heavy-gauge cooking grates, and easy-to-clean surfaces on the interior and exterior of your grill. To keep rain, snow, ice, and sun from ruining your grill, be sure to put a grill cover on it between uses.

Gas grills are convenient and clean. Charcoal grills produce a rich, smoky taste, but require a little more skill at fire-building. The best grill for you depends upon how often you like to grill and the amount of money you have to spend.

Gas Grills

A gas grill may have a gas tank or it may be set up to hook directly to a gas line. The BTU rating (British thermal unit) is a measure of how much gas can flow through the line.

Almost as important as the BTUs of a particular grill is the number of burners. A good gas grill has at least two burners; large grills may have three or more. With more than one burner, you can control the heat more effectively. By turning one or more of the burners off after preheating the grill, you can create the indirect heat necessary to prepare long-cooking foods like a whole turkey or spareribs or delicate foods like breads or vegetables without charring the outside of the food. Most gas grills have covers over the burners. As the foods grill, their juices fall onto this cover and create smoke to flavor the food as it cooks.

The lid for a gas grill should be easy to lift. Keeping the lid closed helps the grill preheat quickly. It also maintains a more even cooking temperature.

If your grill has wheels, be sure that they are sturdy enough to roll over your deck or patio. The grill itself should be sturdy, so if you are shopping for a new grill, give it a shake. It shouldn't wobble or feel loose.

The grease catch should be easy to remove and replace. Be certain that you empty the grease catch often. Otherwise, it will attract unwanted critters.

Weber Genesis Gold gas grill

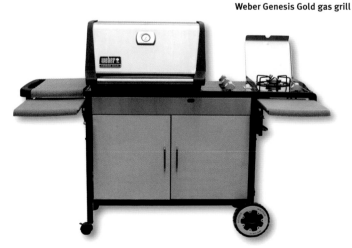

You can find a number of accessories for a gas grill. Some grills have separate burners so you can boil water for corn or steam shellfish while you grill. Some have cutting boards, built-in temperature gauges, adjustable racks, rotisserie units, smokers, or storage. (Some even include refrigerated storage compartments.)

Charcoal Grills

A charcoal grill consists of a base that holds the fire and a cooking rack. The fuel (charcoal briquettes, hardwood chunks, or logs) sits on a grate so that enough oxygen can get to the fuel to help it burn. Some units have vents in the base as well as in the lid to encourage airflow.

Jumbo Joe® charcoal gril

The lid for a charcoal grill helps you control the heat in the grill so that foods cook evenly. It also traps the richly aromatic smoke from the fire. Not all charcoal grills have a lid; for instance, hibachis (sometimes known as braziers) are essentially a cast-iron pan with short feet and a cooking grate. You can tent foods with aluminum foil or a large domed lid from a large pot, if you like.

There are as many bells and whistles available on high-end charcoal grills as there are on high-end gas grills. Some units have electric fire starters, built-in thermostats in the lid to help you monitor how hot the grill is, or propane-fueled side burners.

Smokers

You can get a good smoky flavor in grilled foods without a smoker, but if you enjoy real barbecue, a smoker is your best

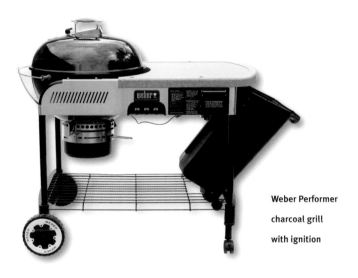

Weber Performer charcoal grill with ignition

Building a Fire in a Charcoal Grill

A good fire burns evenly and lasts long enough to cook everything completely. While gas grills may take as little as 15 minutes to heat up, a fire typically takes at least 35 to 45 minutes before it is ready for cooking.

Lighter fluid and treated charcoal briquettes may be simpler to use, but they can leave a distinct flavor on foods. We strongly recommend avoiding lighter fluid. Never use gasoline or kerosene to start a fire.

To start a fire, open the vents in the grill to let the air in. Crumple a few sheets of newspaper and place them on the fuel grate. Add hardwood chips, briquettes, or kindling to the paper to make a mound, and set the paper on fire. Let it burn, but keep an eye on it. Fires at this stage can go out easily if there is too much or too little air blowing on them. If you are using logs instead of briquettes or chunks, add them once the kindling has started to flame.

Let the fire burn without disturbing it. Add more wood or briquettes carefully when the flames start to die down until you have enough fuel to last for a cooking session.

bet. Barbecued foods are cooked by a technique that is sometimes called "slow and low." The cooking temperature is kept intentionally low so that foods can cook over long periods of time. That gives less-tender cuts like spareribs and brisket plenty of opportunity to cook to a tender, luscious consistency.

Use the same basic guidelines to select a smoker as you would a grill: heavy construction, heavy-gauge metal (usually steel), a tight-fitting lid. In addition, smokers need vents to control the amount of heat and smoke. A built-in temperature gauge makes it possible to control the heat without opening the lid too often. (The more you open the lid, the more smoke is lost.)

There are two types of smokers: vertical water smokers and horizontal dry smokers.

Weber Smokey Mountain Cooker Smoker

Weber Baby-Q

VERTICAL WATER SMOKERS

The barrel of a vertical water smoker is shaped like a bullet. It is usually 2 to 3 feet tall and 18 inches in diameter. These smokers may have an electric or gas heat source located in the bottom of the smoker; some smokers have a chamber where you build a fire from charcoal or wood. To get smoke, wood chunks or chips are added to the heat source. A water pan is positioned above the heat source to maintain gentle, indirect heat throughout the cooking time.

It is important to add wood, water, or charcoal to the smoker as foods cook, so look for some sort of access to the chamber that houses the heat source. Vertical smokers have one or more racks that are suspended above the water pan, and a lid contains the heat and the smoke.

These smokers are typically much smaller and less expensive than other types of smokers.

HORIZONTAL DRY (OR PIT-STYLE) SMOKERS

A horizontal smoker looks more like a barrel that has been laid on its side, cut in half to make a lid, and then set on legs. These smokers are exactly what you would expect to find at a barbecue contest.

There is a large chamber to hold the food as it grills and a second, smaller chamber that holds the fuel. The heat and the smoke from the smaller chamber travels into the larger chamber, and the tight-fitting lid holds in the heat and the smoke.

OPPOSITE, LEFT The briquettes of a properly lit charcoal fire should burn red in the center and have a coating of ash on the outside. The amount of ash on the briquettes directly correlates to the amount of heat they are generating. The thinner the coating of ash, the hotter the fire is. When the coals have an ash coating and are glowing red, spread them in an even layer over the entire grate for direct-heat cooking. If you want to cook foods with indirect head, push them to the side, leaving a space in the center of the fire.

OPPOSITE, RIGHT Move the charcoals to one side to create direct and indirect heat in your charcoal grill.

Some grills have built-in thermometers to make it easy to monitor how hot the grill is. If you don't have such a feature on your grill, you can use a time-honored test:

Hold your hand, palm facing down, over the heat source just above the grill rack. Count how many seconds it takes before you have to take your hand away from the grill.

- ▸ 2 seconds equals high heat
- ▸ 3 seconds equals medium-high heat
- ▸ 4 seconds equals medium heat
- ▸ 5 seconds equals medium-low heat
- ▸ 6 seconds equals low heat

DEALING WITH FLARE-UPS

If flames start to flare up from your burner or the coals while you are grilling, take immediate steps to put out the flames. Move foods away from the flames onto a cooler spot of the grill if possible. Often, the flames will burn out quickly. Once they do, clean the grill rack well.

If the there are just a few small flames but they are not burning out quickly, you can smother them by putting the lid back on a gas grill. If you are using a charcoal grill, put them out by squirting a mist of water from a spray bottle, but don't use this technique for a gas grill.

To keep flames under control once you have had a flare-up, you may need to raise the grill rack, if your racks are adjustable. You can also spread out the coals so that there is a little space between them.

DISPOSING OF COALS

Hot coals can cause fires. Let the coals burn out and cool completely before you remove them from the grill. Use a metal bucket to hold the ashes or wrap them in a double layer of aluminum foil, and don't dump the ashes in with trash that might catch on fire.

Grilling and BBQ Safety

You may be concerned about keeping foods safe when you aren't in your kitchen. Cooking outside means that you are farther away from your refrigerator and your sink. Take steps to be sure that you can keep everything clean and cold, including your hands, while you are grilling. Open flames, hot burners, and combustible materials add to the potential dangers.

Types of Wood for Grilling

You can choose hard wood chunks as a fuel source and chips to use as a flavoring. If you want to get a lot of smoke, soak chips in cold water before you add them to the fire. For a longer-lasting smoke bath, put the chips in an aluminum pan and set the pan directly into the coals or on the side of one of the gas burners (under the grilling rack). In addition to the hard woods listed below, you can use other burnable items: herbs, spices, and teas (bay leaves, rosemary, garlic, mint, orange or lemon peels, whole nutmeg, cinnamon sticks, tea leaves), among others. These vary from spicy (bay leaves or garlic) to sweet, and delicate to mild. Generally, herbs and spices with higher oil content will provide stronger flavoring. Soak branches and stems in water before adding to the fire. They burn quickly, so you may need to replenish often.

WOOD	DESCRIPTION	GOOD WITH
Hickory	Pungent, smoky, baconlike flavor	Pork, chicken, beef, wild game
Pecan	Rich and more subtle than hickory, but similar in taste. Burns cool, so it's ideal for very-low-heat smoking.	Pork, chicken, lamb, fish
Mesquite	Sweeter, more delicate flavor than hickory. Tends to burn hot, so use carefully.	Most meats, especially beef; most vegetables.
Alder	Delicate flavor that enhances lighter meats	Salmon, swordfish, sturgeon, other fish. Also good with chicken and pork.
Oak	Forthright but pleasant flavor. Blends well with a variety of textures and flavors.	Beef (particularly brisket), poultry, pork
Maple	Mildly smoky, somewhat sweet flavor. Try mixing maple with corncobs for grilling ham or bacon. (See below.)	Poultry, vegetables, ham
Cherry	Slightly sweet, fruity smoke flavor	Poultry, game birds, pork
Apple	Slightly sweet but denser, fruity, smoke flavor	Beef, poultry, game birds, pork (particularly ham)
Peach or pear	Slightly sweet, woodsy flavor	Poultry, game birds, pork
Grape vines	Aromatic, similar to fruit woods	Turkey, chicken, beef
Wine barrel chips	Wine and oak flavors. A flavorful novelty that smells wonderful, too.	Beef, turkey, chicken, cheeses
Corncobs	Sweet and smoky flavors. Use corncobs that have had the kernels cut away and break them into pieces. Mix corn cobs with hard woods like maple.	Beef, bacon, ham, or sausage
Seaweed	Tangy and smoky flavors. (Wash and dry in sun before use.)	Lobster, crab, shrimp, mussels, clams

Keep foods either cold or hot. One way to be sure that your food stays properly chilled while you man the grill is to put it into coolers. Be sure that there is plenty of ice or cooling materials. (A single, large block of ice melts more slowly and helps keep foods cool longer.) Take foods directly from the cooler to the grill. Never leave uncooked foods sitting in the sun.

If you aren't going to be close to the sink, bring a container of hot soapy water, a container of plain water, and a clean cloth or sponge to clean off work areas, spatulas, or tongs as you grill. Wash your hands, tools, and containers carefully and as often as needed. Let tools and containers air-dry when possible. If you are using a cutting board to carve grilled foods, be sure that it is thoroughly cleaned and sanitized, especially if you used it to cut up raw foods previously.

Keep foods safe from the sun, bugs, wind, and dust when you are eating alfresco. Try to set up both the area for grilling and the area for eating where your food and your guests will be protected. Domed covers can help keep bugs, leaves, and dirt from landing on your food.

Don't leave foods sitting out for more than two hours, and even less time if the temperature is above 90°F. If you can cool down the foods quickly and get them stored in the refrigerator, they are still good to eat, but if they've gotten warm or been left out for more than 2 hours, discard the foods.

PERSONAL SAFETY

The most common accidents that occur when people grill are burns, but cuts, scrapes, and even falls that result in broken bones or sprains are possible if you aren't careful.

Of course, you'll want to position the grill where it is on a stable, level surface, out of the way of traffic and away from outdoor activities. Any electrical cords should be positioned away from traffic routes so that no one trips over them. Take the following commonsense steps to keep yourself from getting hurt.

- **Never leave the grill unattended.**
- **Don't wear long, loose, flowing clothes when you grill.**
- **Use big oven or grill mitts to protect your hands when lifting heavy items onto or off of the grill.**
- **Never lean over grills or charcoal fires when igniting them.**
- **Use long-handled utensils to turn foods on the grill.**

Grilling and Health Concerns

Recent stories about health and nutrition have noted that there appears to be a connection between grilled foods and cancer. In fact, cooking protein-rich foods like meat, poultry, or seafood at very high temperatures can be a concern. However, like most nutrition advice, the key is moderation. Be moderate not only in how often you eat grilled meats, but also in how dark or charred you let the meat get. A little color is good; in fact, it is the whole point of grilling foods! Too much, though, is more than just a health concern; it is also a culinary concern. Foods that cook until they are charred are bitter and too dry to enjoy.

To minimize the buildup of carbon on meats, fish, and poultry as they grill, remember the following steps:

- *Trim off excess fat.* Fat can melt onto the burner or coals and flare up. Those flames leave sooty deposits on foods.

- *Use marinades.* Some studies have shown that marinating foods before grilling reduces the amount of potentially cancer-causing substances on grilled foods. However, don't use too much marinade. Before grilling foods which have been marinated, let most of the marinade drip away before placing the item on the grill. Most marinades contain oils, and if too much drips onto the burner or coals, they are just as likely to cause flare-ups as the fat from meats and poultry.

- *Use indirect heat to cook meats.* Start meats and other protein-rich foods over direct heat to help them develop a good color, then move them to a cooler part of the grill where flare-ups are less of a concern.

- *Don't eat charred or burned portions of grilled foods.*

- *And, of course, keep the grill rack as clean as possible.*

- Never move a grill when it is hot. Remember that grills stay hot for a long time, even after the coals burn out or the gas is turned off.
- Use baking soda to control small grease flare-ups. Use a fire extinguisher for any flame that doesn't burn out quickly or is too high to control with baking soda. A bucket of sand and a hose are handy to put out flames if you don't have an extinguisher.
- If you do get burned while you are grilling, soak the burn in cool water, but don't apply ice directly to a burn. The ice could damage the tissue.

Grill Safety

Each year, nearly 4,000 fires that cause serious damage and injury are attributed to outdoor grills. To avoid becoming a statistic yourself, clean and maintain grills, propane tanks, electrical accessories, and cords properly.

CLEANING AND MAINTAINING GRILLS

You should clean your grill rack after each grilling session. It's a good idea to scrub the rack again before you start to grill the next time, too. But, there's more to cleaning your grill than making sure there's no buildup of debris on the rack.

Give your grill a thorough cleaning at least twice a year. Your owner's manual will have detailed instructions for cleaning your grill. Do not attempt to clean a grill when it is hot. Once it is cool, brush or scrape away debris or buildup from the inside and outside surfaces of the grill, then wash the inside and outside with clean cloths and soapy water. Rinse with clean water and let the grill dry completely.

To keep gas grills working properly, check the gas fittings for leaks each time you connect or disconnect the gas. To check for leaks, dab the connections with a mixture of soapy water. Next, turn on the gas. If there are bubbles, you've got a leak that must be fixed before you can use the grill again.

Remember to check the tubes connecting propane tanks to the grill frequently. There should be no holes or cracks. Use the same method described above to check for leaks.

Venturi tubes (narrower sections of tube between two wider tubes that function like a pump to draw gas from the tank into the grill) can become clogged. Insects and spiders are common culprits, since they like to build nests in there. If the tubes become blocked, the gas flow becomes uneven and could cause an explosion. Consult your owner's manual to find out how to clean the tubes.

PROPANE CYLINDERS

All propane cylinders manufactured since April 2002 are required to have overfill protection devices (OPD). You can identify these cylinders by the triangular-shaped hand wheel.

Turn off the gas at the cylinder when you are done grilling. Completely close the valve. If you aren't going to be grilling for an extended period, disconnect and safely store the cylinder.

Store propane cylinders outdoors; never store them indoors. Some communities may also have a regulation requiring that these cylinders not be stored on balconies that are more than one floor above the ground.

When you need to transport a cylinder in the car, be sure that the valve is tightly closed. Place the cylinder on the floor behind the passenger's seat. Make sure it can't roll around, and leave the windows rolled down for ventilation. If you must put the cylinder in the trunk of the car, be sure that it is well secured.

Be sure to keep the cylinders in an upright position. This is true whether you are storing the cylinders, using them, or transporting them.

MEATS

Smoky, charred, and gratifying, grilled meats are widely considered to be the ideal main course for meals from the grill. Today's livestock are intentionally bred to be leaner, a nod to our concern with healthy eating. Any chef will tell you, though, that fat equals flavor. The trick to grilling meats successfully is to get enough fat, whether through the meat's own natural marbling or the oils you add to the meat in the form of marinades or basting sauces, to counteract any potential dryness, but without adding so much that the oils make the fire flare up as you cook.

Grilling Temperatures and Times for Meats

Times listed are for medium doneness; cook slightly less for rare, slightly more for medium-well.

Beef steaks (porterhouse, T-bone, sirloin, New York, tenderloin)	¾ inch thick	4 to 5 minutes per side, medium direct heat
	1 inch thick	5 to 6 minutes per side, medium direct heat
	1½ inches thick	8 to 9 minutes per side, start over high direct heat (2 minutes per side), finish with medium indirect heat (6 to 7 minutes more per side)
Beef roasts (loin, sirloin, rib)	5 pounds	1½ to 2 hours total, indirect medium heat
Beef flank steak	¾ inch thick	7 to 8 minutes per side, high direct heat
Beef skirt or hanger steak	½ inch thick	3 to 4 minutes per side, high direct heat
Pork chops from rib, loin, or shoulder	¾ to 1 inch thick	5 to 6 minutes per side, medium direct heat
	1½ inches thick	7 to 8 minutes per side, start over high direct heat (2 minutes per side), finish with medium indirect heat (5 to 6 minutes more per side)
Lamb chops from rib, loin, or shoulder	¾ to 1 inch thick	4 to 6 minutes per side, medium direct heat
Pork tenderloin (whole)		10 to 12 minutes per side, indirect medium heat
Pork ribs (country-style, baby back, spareribs	3 pounds	1½ to 2 hours total, indirect medium heat
Pork or veal roasts (loin, sirloin, rib)	4 pounds	1¼ to 1½ hours total, indirect medium heat
Ground meat patties	¾ inch thick	4 to 5 minutes per side, direct medium heat
	1 inch thick	5 to 6 minutes per side, direct medium heat

ALBUQUERQUE GRILLED PORK TENDERLOIN

with Beans and Greens Sauté

ORK TENDERLOIN cooks quickly over a brisk fire, but you can substitute other meats, as well as poultry and even some fish.

MAKES 6 SERVINGS

3 lbs pork tenderloins

Albuquerque Dry Rub, as needed (page 16)

1 cup pomegranate juice

¼ cup molasses

¼ cup sherry vinegar

Olive oil, as needed

Beans and Greens Sauté (page 17)

1. Blot the tenderloins dry with paper towels. Sprinkle all sides of the tenderloins evenly with some of the dry rub. Cover the tenderloins and refrigerate for at least 2 and up to 12 hours.

2. Preheat a gas grill to medium-high. If you are using a charcoal grill, build a fire and let it burn down until the coals are glowing red with a moderate coating of white ash. Spread the coals in an even bed. Clean the cooking grate.

3. While the grill is heating, make the mop: Simmer the pomegranate juice in a small saucepan over high heat until it reduces by half. Add the molasses and sherry vinegar, stir well, and bring to a simmer. Remove the mop from the heat and reserve 3 tbsp to drizzle on the pork after it is cooked.

4. Brush the tenderloins with a little of the olive oil. Place the tenderloins on the grill and cook until the meat is marked on the first side, about 3 minutes. Turn carefully and brush the upper side of the tenderloins with some of the mop. Turn the tenderloins again when the second side is marked, about 3 minutes, and brush with the mop once again. Grill for another 8 to 9 minutes, covered, then turn once more and brush with mop again. Finish grilling on the second side, covered, until the pork is cooked, another 8 to 9 minutes.

5. Remove the tenderloins from the grill. Allow them to rest for 5 to 10 minutes before slicing. Place slices of the tenderloin on heated plates along with a serving of the Beans and Greens Sauté. Drizzle the reserved mop over the pork slices and serve.

LEFT TO RIGHT Be sure to coat the tenderloins evenly with the dry rub or the flavor will be uneven; you can use gloves if necessary to prevent your hands from getting stained by the dark red rub. Gently turn the pork tenderloins when they are properly marked. Opposite, the Albuquerque Grilled Pork Tenderloin is served with the Beans and Greens Sauté (page 17).

Albuquerque Dry Rub

THIS MAKES enough dry rub to flavor about 3 pounds of meat, fish, or poultry. We suggest starting with whole spices for the best flavor, but you can always substitute ground spices if you prefer.

MAKES ½ CUP DRY RUB

1 tbsp coriander seeds (or 2 tsp ground coriander)

1 tbsp cumin seeds (or 2 tsp ground cumin)

6 tbsp chili powder

1 tbsp onion powder

2 tsp garlic powder

2 tsp dried Mexican oregano

2 tsp salt

½ tsp black peppercorns (or 1 tsp ground pepper)

1. Heat a small sauté pan over medium-high heat. Add the coriander and cumin seeds and toast, swirling the pan constantly, until the seeds give off a rich aroma, about 1 minute. Immediately transfer the seeds to a cool plate and allow to cool for a few minutes.

2. Transfer the seeds to a mortar and pestle or a spice grinder. Add the chili powder, onion and garlic powder, oregano, salt, and pepper. Grind the spices to an even texture. The rub is ready to use now, or you can transfer it to a jar, cover it tightly, and keep it in a cool, dry cupboard or pantry for up to 1 month.

Selecting and Preparing Cuts of Meat for the Grill

You've probably heard that the best meats for grilling are naturally tender. Juicy steaks and chops from the loin or the rib are indeed a good match for the intense dry heat of a grill. The beauty of a grill is that you can control the heat enough to make even tougher cuts a great choice, including veal breast, spareribs, or whole legs of lamb.

SELECT GOOD-QUALITY MEATS

Steaks should be a relatively consistent thickness. Trim any excess fat, but try to leave a thin layer. While you don't want so much fat that it sputters and flares on the grill, a thin, even layer is necessary to prevent the meat from losing moisture and flavor.

ADD A DRY RUB FOR FLAVOR

Rub the mixture evenly over the meat, cover it, and let it sit in the refrigerator for a few hours or even overnight. Shake off the excess before you start to grill it. Otherwise, the rub could scorch. Once that happens, your meat will take on an unpleasant, bitter flavor.

TO ADD MOISTURE TO MEATS, USE AN OIL-BASED MARINADE

Put the meat and the marinade in a heavy-duty resealable bag, seal it tightly, and let the meat marinate in the refrigerator. This method keeps the meat evenly coated in marinade without your having to turn it.

When you take meats out of the marinade, scrape off the excess. Too much oil on the meat will drip down onto the coals or burner. The smoke from the oil could leave sooty deposits on the food.

Beans and Greens Sauté

PREPARE THIS savory sauté in a cast-iron skillet right on the grill while you grill the pork, or make it ahead of time on the stovetop. If you can't find beet greens, substitute spinach, kale, escarole, collard greens, or turnip greens.

MAKES 6 SERVINGS

2 tbsp olive oil

2 tsp minced garlic

10 cups coarsely chopped beet greens

½ cup chicken broth

1 tsp salt, or to taste

½ tsp ground black pepper, or to taste

2 cups cooked or canned cannellini beans, drained and rinsed

2 tsp malt vinegar, or to taste

1. Heat a large sauté pan over the hottest part of the fire or a burner set at medium-high heat. Add the olive oil and heat until the oil shimmers. Add the garlic and move the pan or turn down the heat. Sauté the garlic, stirring frequently, until it is tender and aromatic, about 3 minutes.

2. Add the beet greens and cook, stirring and tossing briskly with a wooden spoon to coat the greens evenly with the oil. When the greens have cooked down and are a vivid green color, add the broth. Season with ½ tsp of the salt and a pinch of the pepper.

3. Bring the broth to a simmer, then add the beans and cook, stirring frequently, until the greens are fully wilted and the dish is very hot. Season to taste with the malt vinegar, salt, and pepper.

You can serve the Beans and Greens Sauté as an accompaniment to a variety of poultry, meats, and fish.

PULLED PORK BARBECUE SANDWICH

MAKES 8 SERVINGS

6 lb pork butt

1 tbsp salt

1 tsp ground black pepper

1 cup Vinegar Barbecue Sauce (recipe follows)

1 cup Black Jack Barbecue Sauce (page 87)

8 sandwich buns, split and toasted

Coleslaw (recipe follows)

1. Preheat a gas grill to medium-low; leave one burner off. If you are using a charcoal grill, build a fire and let it burn down until the coals are glowing red with a heavy coating of white ash. Spread the coals in an even bed on one side of the grill. Clean the cooking grate.

2. Season the pork butt with salt and pepper. Grill, covered, over indirect heat, turning every 15 to 20 minutes, until the meat is completely cooked and very tender, 2½ to 3 hours. Baste the pork with the Vinegar Barbecue Sauce as necessary to keep the meat moistened.

3. Remove the pork from the grill and allow it to cool slightly. When cool enough to handle, pull the pork into shreds. (This can be done up to 2 days in advance.)

4. Combine the pulled pork with the Black Jack Barbecue Sauce in a saucepan over medium-low heat. Heat, stirring gently, until the meat is very hot, about 10 minutes. Serve on the toasted buns with the Coleslaw.

Vinegar Barbecue Sauce

MAKES 4 CUPS

1⅔ cups ketchup

½ cup white vinegar

¼ cup water

¼ cup brown sugar

2 tbsp Worcestershire sauce

4 tsp paprika

4 tsp chili powder

4 tsp dry mustard

1 tsp salt

¾ tsp ground cayenne pepper

Combine all ingredients. Whisk until thoroughly mixed. Serve immediately or store in the refrigerator in a covered container for up to 3 weeks.

Coleslaw

MAKES 8 SERVINGS

6 tbsp sour cream

6 tbsp mayonnaise

3 tbsp cider vinegar

2¼ tsp dry mustard

3 tbsp granulated sugar

1½ tsp celery seeds

1½ tsp Tabasco sauce

Salt, to taste

Ground black pepper, to taste

5 cups shredded green cabbage,

1 cup grated or shredded carrots

1. Mix together the sour cream, mayonnaise, vinegar, mustard, sugar, celery seeds, and Tabasco in a large bowl until smooth. Season the mixture with salt and pepper to taste.

2. Add the cabbage and carrots, and toss until evenly coated. Cover and refrigerate until needed.

BARBECUED SPARERIBS

with Apricot-Ancho Glaze

ANY OF your favorite barbecue sauce recipes (or even bottled barbecue sauce) can make a great sparerib dish, but we really like the sweet, tart, smoky taste and rich golden orange color of the apricot and ancho glaze paired with pork spareribs in this dish. You can also try this glaze with poultry, rabbit, game, veal, and meaty fish like tuna.

MAKES 8 SERVINGS

3 tbsp paprika

½ tsp ground cayenne pepper

1½ tbsp packed brown sugar

¾ tsp dried thyme

4 tsp minced garlic

2¼ tsp salt

2¼ tsp ground black pepper

8 lb pork spareribs

4 cups Apricot-Ancho Barbecue Glaze (recipe follows)

1. Make a rub by combining the paprika, cayenne, sugar, thyme, garlic, salt, and pepper. Rub this mixture generously and evenly over the pork ribs. Place the ribs in a pan, cover, and refrigerate for at least 4 and up to 24 hours before barbecuing.

2. Preheat a gas grill to medium; leave one burner off. If you are using a charcoal grill, build a fire and let it burn down until the coals are glowing red with a moderate coating of white ash. Spread the coals in an even bed on one side of the grill. Clean the cooking grate.

3. Grill the pork ribs over direct heat, covered, until the ribs are browned on both sides, about 15 minutes per side. (If desired, add wood chips to the grill, either directly onto the hot coals or in a small aluminum pan over one of the burners.)

4. Bring the glaze to a simmer in a saucepan; reserve 2 cups of the glaze (and keep warm) to pass with the spareribs. Brush the ribs with a light layer of the remaining barbecue glaze and continue to grill over indirect heat, turning the ribs every 5 to 10 minutes and brushing with sauce after each turn, until the ribs are very tender and a rich glaze has built up on the ribs, another 20 minutes.

5. Remove the pork ribs from the grill and cut into portions. Serve on a heated platter or plates. Pass the reserved barbecue glaze on the side.

Apricot-Ancho Barbecue Glaze

MAKES 4 CUPS

6 strips bacon, chopped

1½ cups small-dice yellow onion

1 tbsp minced garlic

¾ cup ketchup

¾ cup orange juice

¾ cup packed dark brown sugar

⅓ cup chopped dried apricots

¼ cup malt vinegar

2 ancho chiles, diced

1 tsp sweet or hot paprika

1 tsp dry mustard

1 tsp Tabasco sauce

1 tsp ground cayenne pepper

2 tsp salt

1 tsp ground black pepper

1. Sauté the bacon in a large sauté pan over medium heat until almost crisp, about 4 minutes. Add the onions and sauté until browned, about 5 minutes. Add the garlic and sauté until aromatic, about 1 minute.

2. Add all the remaining ingredients. Simmer until the apricots are very soft, about 10 minutes. Taste the sauce and season with additional salt and pepper, if needed.

3. Transfer to a blender and purée until relatively smooth. The glaze is ready to use now, or it can be cooled and stored in a covered container in the refrigerator for up to 1 week.

JERKED PORK CHOPS

J ERK IS a popular type of barbecue in the Caribbean and is most often associated with Jamaica. The seasonings in a jerk blend include allspice along with the habanero or Scotch bonnet chile. The jerk mixture should be like a coarse paste that gets packed onto the meat.

MAKES 8 SERVINGS

2 cups chopped scallions

½ cup olive oil

2 habanero chiles, stemmed and chopped

2 tbsp dried thyme

2 tbsp cider vinegar

1 tbsp ground allspice

1 tbsp ground cinnamon

1½ tsp ground nutmeg

1 tbsp granulated sugar

2 tsp salt

1 tsp ground black pepper

8 boneless pork loin chops, about 1½ inches thick

1. To make the jerk seasoning: Combine the scallions, olive oil, habaneros, thyme, cider vinegar, allspice, cinnamon, nutmeg, sugar, salt, and pepper in a food processor and purée until a coarse paste forms.

2. Spread the jerk seasoning on the pork chops and massage it into the meat (wear gloves to protect your hands). Place in resealable bags and marinate in the refrigerator for at least 4 and up to 12 hours.

3. Preheat a gas grill to high; leave one burner off. If you are using a charcoal grill, build a fire and let it burn down until the coals are glowing red with a light coating of white ash. Spread the coals in an even bed on one side of the grill. Clean the cooking grate.

4. Remove the chops from the bag and brush off any excess marinade. Grill the chops over direct heat for 2 minutes on each side to mark the chops. Move the chops to the cooler side of the grill and continue to grill over medium indirect heat until the pork is completely cooked but still tender, another 5 to 6 minutes per side.

5. Serve on a heated platter or plates.

GUAVA-GLAZED BABY BACK RIBS

BABY BACK ribs are meatier and less fatty than spareribs. They are sold in racks that may be whole, halved, or quartered when you buy them. Keep an eye on these ribs as they cook, since the danger of overcooking is significant with baby back ribs.

MAKES 8 SERVINGS

2½ cups water

1½ cups red wine vinegar

1½ cups chopped oregano leaves

1¼ cups chopped cilantro leaves

1 cup chopped yellow onion

8 garlic cloves, minced

2 tsp ground cumin

1½ tsp ground black pepper

8 lb pork baby back ribs

4 cups Guava Barbecue Sauce (recipe follows)

1. Make a marinade by puréeing the water, vinegar, oregano, cilantro, onion, garlic, cumin, and pepper in a blender.

2. Place the ribs in a large container and coat with the marinade. Cover and refrigerate for at least 24 and up to 36 hours.

3. Preheat a gas grill to medium; leave one burner off. If you are using a charcoal grill, build a fire and let it burn down until the coals are glowing red with a moderate coating of white ash. Spread the coals in an even bed on one side of the grill. Clean the cooking grate.

4. Grill the pork ribs over indirect heat, covered, until the ribs are browned on both sides, about 15 minutes per side. (If desired, add wood chips to the grill, either directly onto the hot coals or in a small aluminum pan over one of the burners.)

5. Bring the barbecue sauce to a simmer in a saucepan; reserve 2 cups of the sauce (and keep warm) to pass with the spareribs. Brush the ribs with a light coating of the barbecue sauce and continue to barbecue over indirect heat, turning the ribs every 5 minutes and brushing with sauce after each turn, until the ribs are very tender and a rich glaze has built up on the ribs, another 30 to 35 minutes.

6. Remove the pork ribs from the grill and cut into portions. Serve on a heated platter or plates. Pass the reserved barbecue sauce on the side.

Guava Barbecue Sauce

MAKES 4 CUPS

1½ cups guava marmalade

1 cup water

½ cup dry sherry wine

¼ cup tomato paste

2 tbsp dry mustard

4 tsp molasses

1 habanero chile, minced

5 tsp minced garlic

1 tbsp ground cumin

2 tsp salt

1 tsp ground black pepper

½ cup lime juice

1. Combine all of the ingredients except for the lime juice in a saucepan. Simmer the sauce until slightly thickened, about 30 minutes.

2. Remove from the heat and stir in the lime juice. The sauce is ready to use now, or it can be cooled and stored in a covered container in the refrigerator for up to 1 week.

SKEWERED BEEF FILLET

with Chimichurri Sauce

CHIMICHURRI SAUCE is a ubiquitous oil-and-vinegar–based condiment from Argentina, where it is served with grilled meats as well as a variety of other dishes. This fresh-tasting sauce is a nice alternative to traditional barbecue sauces.

MAKES 8 SERVINGS

8 bamboo skewers, 8 inches long

2 tsp salt

8 garlic cloves, minced

½ cup finely diced red pepper

¼ cup minced yellow onion

¼ cup minced parsley leaves

¼ cup minced oregano leaves

½ cup finely diced tomato

2 jalapeños, minced

¼ cup water

¼ cup extra-virgin olive oil

¼ cup red wine vinegar

4 strip steaks, ½ inch thick

½ tsp ground black pepper

1. Soak the bamboo skewers in cool water for at least 30 minutes.

2. Sprinkle 1 tsp of the salt over the minced garlic and mash to a paste with the flat side of a chef's knife.

3. Transfer the garlic to a nonreactive bowl and add the red pepper, onion, parsley, oregano, tomato, jalapenos, water, extra-virgin olive oil, and red wine vinegar. Mix well and refrigerate for 1 hour to let the flavors blend.

4. Preheat a gas grill to high. If you are using a charcoal grill, build a fire and let it burn down until the coals are glowing red with a light coating of white ash. Spread the coals in an even bed. Clean the cooking grate.

5. Trim the steaks of excess fat. Cut the steaks into strips about 1½ inches wide and thread the strips onto the bamboo skewers. Season the meat with the remaining salt and pepper.

6. Grill the beef to desired doneness, about 2 minutes per side for medium-rare.

7. Serve the beef hot with the cold chimichurri sauce.

BEEF STRIP LOIN WITH WILD MUSHROOM RUB

and Wild Mushroom Sauté

IF TRI-TIP is available in your local meat market, try that cut instead of the strip loin shown here. The Wild Mushroom Rub pairs well with beef, veal, and game. Try it on fish, like halibut or sea bass, as well.

MAKES 8 SERVINGS

3 lb boneless beef strip loin

½ cup Wild Mushroom Rub (recipe follows)

¼ cup peanut oil

Wild Mushroom Sauté (page 26)

1. Clean and trim the strip loin. Rub the dry rub evenly over the entire surface of the meat; cover and refrigerate for at least 3 and up to 12 hours.

2. Preheat a gas grill to medium; leave one burner off. If you are using a charcoal grill, build a fire and let it burn down until the coals are glowing red with a moderate coating of white ash. Spread the coals in an even bed on one side of the grill. Clean the cooking grate.

3. Brush the beef with the oil. Grill the beef over indirect heat, covered, turning every 15 to 20 minutes, until the beef is medium-rare, about 1 hour. (If desired, add dampened wood chips to the grill, either directly onto hot coals or in a small aluminum pan over one of the burners.)

4. Allow the beef to rest for 10 minutes before slicing. Serve the slices on heated plates or a platter with the Wild Mushroom Sauté.

Wild Mushroom Rub

MAKES ½ CUP

2 oz assorted dried mushrooms (about 2 cups)

1 tsp garlic powder

1 tsp onion powder

1 tsp paprika

1 tsp dried thyme

¼ tsp ground cumin

1 tsp salt

¼ tsp ground black pepper

1. Grind the mushrooms in a spice grinder or blender to an even texture. Transfer to a bowl and stir in the garlic and onion powders, paprika, thyme, cumin, salt, and pepper.

2. The rub is ready to use now, or you can transfer it to a jar, cover it tightly, and keep it in a cool, dry cupboard or pantry for up to 1 month.

The Beef Strip Loin with Wild Mushroom Rub and Wild Mushroom Sauté is served here with Skillet Cornbread (page 150).

Wild Mushroom Sauté

REMEMBER TO cook the mushrooms in batches to achieve a proper golden brown color. Once you add the rest of the ingredients, keep everything moving to prevent burning, or try reducing the fire to moderate heat.

MAKES 8 SERVINGS

¼ cup peanut oil

2 lb assorted mushrooms, large-diced

¼ cup minced shallots

2 tsp minced garlic

3 tbsp chopped parsley

2 tbsp butter

½ tsp salt

¼ tsp pepper

1. Heat the oil in a sauté pan over high heat until smoking. Add the mushrooms to the pan in batches and sauté until golden, about 5 to 7 minutes.

2. Add the shallots, garlic, parsley, and butter; stir to blend, and sauté until aromatic and very hot, about 2 minutes more. Season to taste with the salt and pepper.

3. The mushroom sauté is ready to use now or it can be cooled and stored in a covered container in the refrigerator for up to 2 days.

About Mushrooms

Mushrooms exist in thousands of varieties, ranging significantly in size, shape, color, and flavor. For a long time, the only widely available mushrooms were white mushrooms (also sold as button mushrooms or Parisian mushrooms). Today, more varieties are being successfully farmed, which means that many so-called "wild" varieties are actually farm-raised.

Europeans, especially those living in the eastern and northern parts of the continent, are inveterate mushroom hunters. It isn't at all unusual to find whole families engaged in a hunt through the woods on a Sunday afternoon. Foraging for wild food used to be common in this country too, but if you aren't familiar with the local flora and fauna, it is probably safest to err on the side of caution. If you aren't sure about a wild mushroom's safety, don't sauté it and serve it for dinner. Contact local agricultural groups or even a community college agricultural program to locate an expert who can help you identify your mushrooms.

- Cultivated mushroom varieties include white mushrooms, as well as portobello, cremini, shiitake, and oyster mushrooms.

- Wild mushroom varieties include cèpes (porcini), chanterelles, morels, truffles, and many other varieties.

- Select mushrooms that are firm, without soft spots, blemishes, or breaks in the cap or stem.

- Keep mushrooms under refrigeration. Cover with lightly dampened paper towels, not plastic wrap, to keep them fresher long.

- Keep mushrooms as dry as possible until ready to cook.

BEEF TERIYAKI

TERIYAKI IS a Japanese style of grilling. The word *teri-yaki* comes from two Japanese words: *teri,* which means shiny or lustrous, and *yaki,* which means grill. The meat is cut into thin strips and marinated. You could substitute molasses, maple syrup, or brown sugar for the honey in the marinade.

MAKES 8 SERVINGS

¾ cup soy sauce

¾ cup peanut oil

¼ cup dry sherry wine

2 tbsp grated orange zest, optional

4 tsp honey

1 tbsp minced garlic

1 tbsp grated ginger

8 beef tenderloin steaks, about ¾ inch thick

1¼ cups Teriyaki Sauce (recipe follows)

1. Combine the soy sauce, peanut oil, sherry, orange zest (if using), honey, garlic, and ginger in a resealable bag. Add the tenderloin steaks and seal the bag, pressing out the air. Marinate the beef in the refrigerator for at least 2 and up to 8 hours.

2. Preheat a gas grill to medium-high. If you are using a charcoal grill, build a fire and let it burn down until the coals are glowing red with a moderate coating of white ash. Spread the coals in an even bed. Clean the cooking grate.

3. Grill the steaks over direct heat until medium-rare, about 3 to 4 minutes on each side. Serve the beef at once on a heated platter or plates. Pass the teriyaki sauce on the side.

Teriyaki Sauce

MIRIN IS a clear, amber-colored Japanese sweet rice wine made from fermented sweet rice (*mochi-game*), a yeast (*koji*), and a Japanese liquor (*sho-chu*). It is a key ingredient in teriyaki sauce, where it adds a delicate note of sweetness and a touch of acidity. Good-quality mirin, sold as *hon-mirin,* is made according to traditional, and time-consuming, techniques that result in a thickened, syrupy liquid with a wonderful aroma and taste that commands a price comparable to that of a good quality sake. Cheaper varieties are available, but they won't have the complex flavor of a good mirin.

MAKES 1¼ CUPS

2 tbsp cornstarch

2 tbsp cold water

¾ cup chicken broth

⅓ cup tamari sauce

¼ cup minced green onions

2 tbsp sake

2 tbsp mirin (sweet rice wine)

2 tbsp granulated sugar

1 tbsp rice vinegar

1 tsp minced ginger

1 tsp minced garlic

1. Combine the cornstarch and the cold water, and stir until smooth. Set aside.

2. Simmer the broth, tamari sauce, green onions, sake, mirin, sugar, rice vinegar, ginger, and garlic until the flavors combine, about 15 minutes.

3. Stir the cornstarch mixture to recombine, and add it to the simmering sauce a bit at a time, stirring continuously, adding just enough to thicken the sauce so that it lightly coats the back of a spoon. Keep the sauce warm until ready to serve. Or, cool the sauce and store it in a covered container in the refrigerator for up to 3 days.

BISTECCA ALLA FIORENTINA

(Grilled T-Bone Steak Tuscan-Style)

A FINAL DRIZZLE of good olive oil and a squirt of fresh lemon juice gives this steak its Florentine flavor. Each steak serves two. To carve the steaks, cut the meat from the bone with the tip of your knife; it will separate easily and cleanly from the bones if you use short strokes and keep the blade as close to the bone as you can. Once you've cut the meat free, carve it into slices.

MAKES 8 SERVINGS

4 T-bone steaks, 1½ inches thick

¼ cup extra-virgin olive oil, divided use

¼ cup minced garlic

4 tsp salt

2 tsp ground black pepper

2 tsp minced rosemary leaves

3 tbsp lemon juice

1. Preheat a gas grill to high; leave one burner off. If you are using a charcoal grill, build a fire and let it burn down until the coals are glowing red with a light coating of white ash. Spread the coals in an even bed on one side of the grill. Clean the cooking grate.

2. Brush the steaks with a bit of the oil and season generously with the garlic, salt, pepper, and rosemary.

3. Grill the steaks over direct heat until marked, about 2 minutes on each side. Move the steaks to the cooler part of the grill and continue to grill over indirect medium heat until medium-rare, another 6 to 7 minutes on each side.

4. Transfer the meat to a cutting board or a large platter. Drizzle each of the steaks with 2 tsp more olive oil and finish by sprinkling the steaks with lemon juice.

5. Let the steaks rest for about 10 to 15 minutes before carving into slices. Serve on a heated platter or plates.

The steak is carved, cut into slices, and then served with the bone for an attractive presentation that makes it easy for people to serve themselves. The Bistecca alla Fiorentina is served here with Creamy Polenta (see note in the recipe for Grilled Herbed Polenta, page 148).

GRILLED BEEF FAJITAS

THIS RECIPE is easy to adjust to make into a cozy dinner for two or for a large backyard party.

MAKES 8 SERVINGS

5 lb flank steak, ¾ inch thick

4 tsp salt

2¼ tsp ground black pepper

1½ cups lime juice

3 tbsp minced garlic

¾ cup minced yellow onion

2 tbsp olive oil

2 red peppers, cut into thin strips

2 green peppers, cut into thin strips

2 yellow peppers, cut into thin strips

½ red onion, sliced

16 corn or flour tortillas, 6 inches in diameter

1. Trim the meat to remove any visible fat. Combine the salt, pepper, lime juice, garlic, and minced onion. Marinate the flank steak for at least 2 and up to 24 hours.

2. Preheat a gas grill to high. If you are using a charcoal grill, build a fire and let it burn down until the coals are glowing red with a light coating of white ash. Spread the coals in an even bed. Clean the cooking grate.

3. Grill the steaks for 7 to 8 minutes per side for medium, or grill to desired doneness. Remove the steaks from the grill and allow them to cool. Cut the steaks into ¼-inch-thick strips.

4. In a large sauté pan, heat the olive oil over medium heat. Sauté the peppers and onions for 5 to 7 minutes, or until they just begin to soften. Add the steak and cook until just heated through, about 2 to 3 minutes.

5. Grill the tortillas until softened and warm, about 20 seconds per side.

6. Serve the fajita mixture with the tortillas and a variety of toppings, such as cheese, sour cream, Guacamole (page 35), or Chipotle Pico de Gallo (page 72).

GRILLED VENISON CHOPS

with Sherry-Mustard Sauce

YOU MAY be able to find venison in specialty grocery stores or in a traditional butcher shop. Try emu or ostrich instead of venison, if you have a source for those meats.

MAKES 8 SERVINGS

6 tbsp vegetable oil, or as needed

1½ cups minced green onions

6 tbsp minced shallots

¼ cup sherry vinegar

¼ cup Dijon-style mustard

8 tbsp honey

2 cups chicken broth

2 cups heavy cream

½ cup sherry wine

4 tsp chopped rosemary

Salt, as needed

Ground black pepper, as needed

8 venison loin chops, 7 to 8 oz each

1. To prepare the sherry-mustard sauce: Heat 4 tablespoons of the oil in a saucepan over medium-high heat. Add the green onions and shallots; sauté, stirring frequently, until tender, about 4 minutes. Add the sherry vinegar and cook until reduced, 3 to 4 minutes. Add the mustard and honey, and cook until aromatic, 30 to 40 seconds.

2. Add the broth and heavy cream; simmer until reduced by half, about 10 minutes. Add the sherry wine and rosemary, and continue to simmer until heated through. Add salt and pepper to taste.

3. The sauce is ready to serve now or it can be cooled and stored in the refrigerator for up to 3 days. (Bring the sauce to a simmer over high heat before serving.)

4. Preheat a gas grill to high; leave one burner off. If you are using a charcoal grill, build a fire and let it burn down until the coals are glowing red with a light coating of white ash. Spread the coals in an even bed on one side of the grill. Clean the cooking grate.

5. Season the chops generously with salt and pepper and brush lightly with the remaining oil.

6. Grill the chops over high heat until well-colored, 3 minutes. Turn once and continue to cook over direct high heat until browned, another 3 minutes. Move the chops to indirect medium heat, turning them as you move them. Finish grilling the chops to the desired doneness, about 2 to 3 minutes more per side (depending upon the thickness of the chops, heat of grill, and desired doneness).

7. Serve the chops on heated plates with the sauce.

Although we used venison loin chops, you can substitute venison rack chops to make a dramatic presentation similar to rack of lamb. The Grilled Venison Chops with Sherry-Mustard Sauce is served here with the Grilled Sweet Potatoes with Pecan-Molasses Butter (page 147) and Grilled Asparagus and Sweet Peppers (page 123).

PAKISTANI-STYLE LAMB PATTIES

PINE NUTS, oregano, garlic, and lamb combine in these savory patties for a delicious Middle Eastern–inspired burger. Toast the pine nuts in a small, dry skillet over medium heat. Swirl the pan while the pine nuts toast. As they heat up, they'll become shiny, indicating that they will quickly start to turn brown. As soon as the nuts are just slightly paler than you like, pour them out of the pan into a cool bowl.

MAKES 8 SERVINGS

6 tbsp fresh white breadcrumbs

¼ cup cold water

2 tbsp vegetable oil

3 tbsp minced yellow onion

1½ tsp minced garlic

2½ lb lean ground lamb

2 eggs, lightly beaten

3 tbsp toasted pine nuts

3 tbsp chopped parsley

2 tbsp tahini

2 tbsp grated ginger

2 tbsp ground cumin

¾ tsp ground coriander

¾ tsp ground fennel seeds

1½ tsp salt

¾ tsp ground black pepper

1. Soak the breadcrumbs in the water until well moistened, about 2 minutes. Squeeze out any excess moisture. Transfer to a bowl.

2. Heat the oil in a sauté pan over medium-high heat. Add the onion and sauté, stirring frequently, until translucent, about 4 to 5 minutes. Add the garlic and sauté until aromatic, about 1 minute. Remove from heat and transfer to a plate to cool.

3. Combine the breadcrumbs and the onion-garlic mixture with the lamb, eggs, pine nuts, parsley, tahini, ginger, cumin, coriander, fennel, salt, and pepper. Mix gently until the ingredients are evenly blended.

4. Shape the mixture into 8 patties about 4 inches in diameter and ¾ inch thick, and chill them in the refrigerator.

5. Preheat a gas grill to medium-high. If you are using a charcoal grill, build a fire and let it burn down until the coals are glowing red with a moderate coating of white ash. Spread the coals in an even bed. Clean the cooking grate.

6. Grill the patties over direct heat until medium, about 4 to 5 minutes on each side.

Grinding Meats

You may not find ground lamb in the meat case at your local market. You can grind your own lamb and other meats, if you have a meat grinder or grinding attachments for a stand mixer.

Select a boneless roast from the shoulder or the leg and trim away as much of the fat as you can. Since you need to cut the meat into pieces before you can grind it, you can locate any pockets of fat on the interior of the meat and cut them out too.

Cut larger pieces into thin strips or small cubes that will drop through the opening in the top of the grinder, and then chill the meat while you get the grinder ready.

Be sure that all grinder pieces are very clean and chilled. (You can put them in the freezer for a while or put them in a bowl filled with ice water.) Put all the pieces together and set a clean, cold bowl under the opening on the grinder to catch the meat as it falls.

Drop the meat through the opening in the top with the grinder running, but don't try to add too much at once. The strips or cubes should fall easily through the tube. Keep grinding until all of the meat is finished.

After you are done, take the grinder apart, wash it, and let all the pieces dry thoroughly before putting it away.

GRILLED HAMBURGERS

with Guacamole and Chipotle Pico de Gallo

YOU CAN substitute jalapeño Jack cheese for the caciotta if it is unavailable in your neighborhood grocery store.

MAKES 8 SERVINGS

3 lb ground beef

6 tbsp dry panko (Japanese-style breadcrumbs)

2 tbsp salt

1 tbsp ground black pepper

2 tsp ground cumin, optional

8 slices caciotta cheese

8 hamburger buns or Kaiser rolls

1 cup Chipotle Pico de Gallo (page 72)

1 cup Guacamole (recipe follows)

8 Boston lettuce leaves, optional

16 slices tomato, optional

8 slices red onion (grilled, if desired), optional

1. Preheat a gas grill to medium-high. If you are using a charcoal grill, build a fire and let it burn down until the coals are glowing red with a moderate coating of white ash. Spread the coals in an even bed. Clean the cooking grate.

2. While the grill is heating, combine the ground beef with the breadcrumbs, salt, pepper, and cumin. Shape into 8 patties about 4 inches in diameter and ¾ inch thick.

3. Grill the beef until well marked, about 4 to 6 minutes. Flip the burgers over and grill until cooked through, about 4 minutes for medium, 6 minutes for medium-well.

4. Place the cheese on the burgers the last 2 minutes of grilling and allow it to melt. Place the burgers on the buns.

5. Serve the burgers dressed with the Pico de Gallo, Guacamole, lettuce, tomato, and onion.

Guacamole

MAKES 2 CUPS

¼ cup small-dice red onion

3 ripe avocados, peeled and diced roughly

⅓ cup small-dice plum tomatoes

1 tbsp minced jalapeño pepper, or to taste

1 tbsp chopped cilantro

3 tbsp lime juice

1½ tsp salt

½ tsp ground black pepper

3 dashes Tabasco

1. Soak the red onion in cold water for 20 minutes; this will mellow their flavor. Drain and rinse.

2. Combine all the ingredients and mix well. Smash the avocados a little to form a rough paste as you mix it all together. Refrigerate until ready to use. Guacamole can be stored in a covered container in the refrigerator for up to 8 hours.

GRILLED LAMB CHOPS

with Artichoke and Tomato Sauté

THIS RECIPE works for both loin and rib chops. To French the rib chops, scrape the section of bone past the medallion of meat with the blade of a knife until the bone is clean.

MAKES 8 SERVINGS

6 tbsp olive oil

3 tbsp lemon juice

3 tbsp soy sauce

1 tbsp chopped thyme

16 lamb chops, rib or loin, about 3 oz each, ¾ to 1 inch thick

Salt, to taste

Ground black pepper, to taste

Artichoke and Tomato Sauté (recipe follows)

1. Combine the oil, lemon juice, soy sauce, and thyme. Place the lamb chops on a platter and pour the marinade over the chops. Cover and let marinate in the refrigerator for 1 to 2 hours.

2. Preheat a gas grill to medium-high. If you are using a charcoal grill, build a fire and let it burn down until the coals are glowing red with a moderate coating of white ash. Spread the coals in an even bed. Clean the cooking grate.

3. Drain the lamb chops and season with salt and pepper.

4. Grill the lamb chops over direct heat until medium, about 4 to 6 minutes on each side.

5. Serve the lamb chops on a heated platter over the Artichoke and Tomato Sauté.

Artichoke and Tomato Sauté

TO CUT zucchini into julienne, first cut ¼-inch-thick strips from the outside of the zucchini, leaving behind the seeds. (You can discard this part of the zucchini without feeling guilty; there really isn't a lot of nutritional value to be found there.) Cut the strips into 2-inch-long pieces and then cut the pieces into thin strips.

MAKES 8 SERVINGS

¼ cup olive oil

½ cup minced shallot

2 tsp minced garlic

4 cups zucchini julienne

¾ cup diced tomato

8 sliced artichoke bottoms (see below)

2¼ tsp chopped pepperoncini

1½ tsp salt

¾ tsp ground black pepper

Heat the olive oil in a sauté pan over medium heat; add the shallot and garlic, and sauté until aromatic, about 2 minutes. Add the zucchini, and continue to sauté until the zucchini wilts and becomes tender, 5 to 6 minutes. Add the tomato and artichoke bottoms and continue to sauté, stirring as necessary, until very hot, another 3 to 4 minutes. Stir in the pepperoncini and season with salt and pepper. Serve at once or keep warm for up to 1 hour.

Artichokes

Artichoke bottoms are the meatiest part of the artichoke. You can find them packed in brine in the canned goods aisle, or even in the freezer section. But they are not difficult to prepare from fresh artichokes and the difference in texture is worth the added steps.

Select artichokes with leaves that are tightly attached. The stem should look firm, with no big splits or cracks. Before you start cutting your artichokes, cut a lemon in half. The acid in the lemon juice will keep the artichoke from turning brown after you cut it. And then, you can add the lemon to the pot when you cook the artichokes, both to maintain a good color in the artichokes and flavor them.

Use a heavy-duty chef's knife to cut through the leaves about 2 inches from the top of the artichoke. This will expose the light colored inner leaves. Use a paring knife or kitchen scissors to trim the leaves at the base of the stem.

(You can choose to cut the remaining leaves away now and discard them or trim the barbs from each leaf but leave them attached to the artichoke. If you leave them in place, you can cut them away after you simmer the artichoke and enjoy them with a dipping sauce.)

Once the bottoms are trimmed, use a serving spoon to scoop out the tiny white or purple leaves at the center of the artichoke as well as the downy hair that covers the artichoke bottom.

Cook the artichoke bottoms in a pot of simmering water along with a dash of lemon juice and salt to taste. Most artichokes will be tender after simmering 10 to 12 minutes, but very small artichokes won't take as long, while bigger varieties will take longer. Test them for doneness the same way you would a potato; the tip of a knife should slide into them easily.

Drain the artichokes and use them in a recipe as directed, or store them in a container, covered with some of the cooking liquid and covered tightly, for up to 5 days.

SPICY LAMB KEBABS

with Pickled Grapes

THE FLAVORS in this recipe are largely inspired by Greek cooking, but with the distinct influence of Asian cuisine as well, blending the refreshing bite of fresh herbs with the pungency of cinnamon and ginger, and the brilliant colors of saffron and turmeric.

MAKES 8 SERVINGS

3 lb boneless leg of lamb

5 tbsp minced garlic

¼ cup olive oil

¼ cup lemon juice

4 tsp minced flat-leaf parsley

2 tbsp minced oregano leaves

1 tbsp ground coriander

2 tsp minced ginger

2 tsp Spanish-style paprika

2 tsp salt

1 tsp ground black pepper

½ tsp ground turmeric

½ tsp ground cayenne pepper

¼ tsp crushed saffron threads

16 bamboo skewers

32 Pickled Grapes (recipe follows)

1. Trim the lamb and cut it into 1-inch cubes; you should have about 48 pieces.

2. Thoroughly combine all the remaining ingredients except

As a variation, try substituting other meats like pork, rabbit, or venison for the lamb, to create a sweet and slightly spicy meal that is sure to intrigue your guests.

the grapes. Coat the meat evenly with the mixture. Cover and marinate in the refrigerator for at least 2 and up to 12 hours.

3. Remove the lamb from the refrigerator 30 minutes before grilling. Soak the bamboo skewers in cool water for 30 minutes. Drain just before using.

4. Preheat a gas grill to medium-high. If you are using a charcoal grill, build a fire and let it burn down until the coals are glowing red with a moderate coating of white ash. Spread the coals in an even bed. Clean the cooking grate.

5. While the grill is heating, thread 3 pieces of meat and 2 grapes on each skewer. Grill until medium-rare, 2 to 3 minutes on each side. Serve at once.

Pickled Grapes

MAKES 2½ CUPS

1½ cups granulated sugar

¾ cup white wine vinegar

1 cinnamon stick

¼ tsp salt

1¼ cups seedless green grapes (about 32 grapes)

1¼ cups seedless black grapes (about 32 grapes)

1. Combine the sugar, vinegar, cinnamon stick, and salt in a saucepan. Simmer over medium heat until the sugar has completely dissolved, about 5 minutes.

2. Pour the mixture over the grapes, and allow the grapes to cool to room temperature. Refrigerate overnight, covered. The grapes are ready to use now or they can be stored in the refrigerator for up to 2 weeks.

RAZNJICI

(Pork and Veal Skewers)

THESE EASTERN European skewers combine pork, veal, onions, and dill. Grilled onions would be a perfect companion, along with chunks of pumpernickel bread.

MAKES 8 SERVINGS

8 bamboo skewers

1½ lb boneless veal top round

1½ lb boneless pork loin

Salt, to taste

Ground black pepper, to taste

6 tbsp thinly sliced garlic

1 cup thinly sliced yellow onion

6 tbsp vegetable oil

6 tbsp lemon juice

2 tbsp chopped parsley

Dill Sauce (recipe follows)

1. Soak the bamboo skewers in cool water for 30 minutes.

2. Cut the veal and pork into 1½-inch cubes, pat dry, and season with salt and pepper. Thread the meat onto the soaked bamboo skewers.

3. Combine the remaining ingredients except the Dill Sauce. Pour the mixture over the meat. Cover and marinate for at least 3 hours or up to overnight in the refrigerator.

4. Preheat a gas grill to medium-high. If you are using a charcoal grill, build a fire and let it burn down until the coals are glowing red with a moderate coating of white ash. Spread the coals in an even bed. Clean the cooking grate.

5. Allow excess marinade to drain from the meat before grilling; blot with paper towels if necessary. Reserve the marinade and boil in a saucepan for 3 minutes; keep warm. Place the meat on the grill, and grill undisturbed for about 3 to 4 minutes. Turn the skewers over and grill about 3 to 4 minutes more. Brush the meat with the warm marinade as it grills. Serve with the Dill Sauce.

Dill Sauce

MAKES 8 SERVINGS

5 tbsp butter

6 tbsp all-purpose flour

5 cups chicken broth, hot

Salt, to taste

Ground black pepper, to taste

¾ cup sour cream

3 tbsp chopped dill

1. Melt the butter in a large saucepan over low heat, then whisk in the flour. Cook over low heat, whisking constantly, until smooth and pale golden in color to make a blond roux.

2. Add the hot broth to the roux and bring to a boil. Reduce to a simmer and cook, uncovered, for about 45 minutes, or as long as needed to make a smooth, flavorful velouté sauce. Skim off any fat that rises to the top and adjust seasoning with salt and pepper to taste throughout simmering time.

3. Strain the velouté through a fine-mesh sieve and return to low heat. Stir about 1 cup of the velouté into the sour cream and add it back into the sauce. Add the dill. Return to just below a simmer; adjust seasoning to taste. Serve the sauce warm. If the sauce is made in advance, it can be cooled and stored in a covered container in the refrigerator for up to 3 days. Warm the sauce over low heat until it reaches a simmer before serving.

BARBECUED VEAL BREAST

THE VEAL breasts sold bone-in have about 5 rib bones, with lots of meat. Once the veal breast is cooked, you can cut the riblets away if you like. Cut between each rib down to the bone that connects all the ribs, and with the tip of your knife, cut the rib away. There's a large nugget of meat along the end opposite the tips of the ribs; pull or cut the meat away to enjoy now, or later on as a pulled veal sandwich.

MAKES 8 SERVINGS

1 cup apple cider vinegar

1 cup apple cider or apple juice

¼ cup Worcestershire sauce

2 tsp Tabasco sauce

¼ cup lightly packed brown sugar

4 tsp minced garlic

2 tbsp salt

6 lb veal breasts, trimmed and silverskin removed

3 cups Barbecue Sauce (recipe follows)

1. Combine all the ingredients except the veal and Barbecue Sauce in a mixing bowl and whisk to blend.

2. Place the veal breasts in a large pan and pour the mixture over the meat. Let marinate in the refrigerator, covered, for at least 8 and up to 24 hours.

3. Preheat a gas grill to low. Leave one burner off. If you are using a charcoal grill, build a fire and let it burn down until the coals are glowing red with a very heavy coating of white ash. Push the coals to one side of the grill. Clean the cooking grate.

4. Remove the veal breasts from the marinade, letting any excess marinade run off. Pat the meat dry with paper towels.

5. Grill the veal breasts over indirect heat, covered, until the veal is browned on both sides, turning the meat every 15 to 20 minutes, about 2 hours.

6. Brush the veal breasts with an even layer of the Barbecue Sauce, turn, and continue to grill over indirect heat. Brush with a light layer of the barbecue sauce and turn every 20 minutes, continuing to grill over indirect heat until the veal is very tender and a rich glaze has built up on the veal breasts, another 2 to 2½ hours.

7. Remove the veal breasts from the grill and cut or pull the meat from the bones. Pass any remaining Barbecue Sauce on the side.

Barbecue Sauce

MAKES 3 CUPS

1⅔ cups ketchup

½ cup white vinegar

¼ cup water

¼ cup packed brown sugar

2 tbsp Worcestershire sauce

4½ tsp paprika

4½ tsp chili powder

4½ tsp dry mustard

1 tsp salt

¾ tsp ground cayenne pepper

Combine all the ingredients in a mixing bowl. Whisk until thoroughly mixed. Serve immediately or store in the refrigerator for up to 3 weeks.

BERBERE GRILLED LEG OF LAMB

THE COOKING time suggested here should produce a nice rare doneness, not bloody. However, it is hard to gauge how fast things will cook over indirect heat, so it is important to use an accurate meat thermometer.

MAKES 8 SERVINGS

1 leg of lamb, boneless roast, about 3 lb

1½ tsp salt

¾ tsp coarse-ground black pepper

¼ cup olive oil

¼ cup slivered garlic

½ cup Berbere Spice Paste (page 44)

Grilled Potato and Red Onion Fans (page 156)

Grilled Leeks (page 144)

1. Unroll the leg of lamb and make cuts as necessary to butterfly the leg (see note on page 44). It should be an even thickness throughout, about 1½ to 1¾ inches. Blot dry with paper towels and season with salt and pepper. Brush the top with half of the olive oil, sprinkle with half of the garlic, and spread with half of the spice paste. Turn the lamb over and repeat with the remaining oil, garlic, and spice paste.

2. Marinate the lamb, covered, in the refrigerator for at least 6 and up to 12 hours.

3. Preheat a gas grill to medium-high. Leave one burner off. If you are using a charcoal grill, build a fire and let it burn down until the coals are glowing red with a moderate coating of white ash. Push the coals to one side of the grill. Clean the cooking grate.

4. Grill the lamb over direct heat until marked, about 3 minutes on each side. Move the lamb to the cool side of the grill. Continue to cook, turning every 15 minutes, until desired doneness is reached, about 1 hour and 10 minutes for medium-rare.

5. Remove the lamb from the grill and allow it to rest at least 10 minutes before slicing. Serve with the potatoes and leeks.

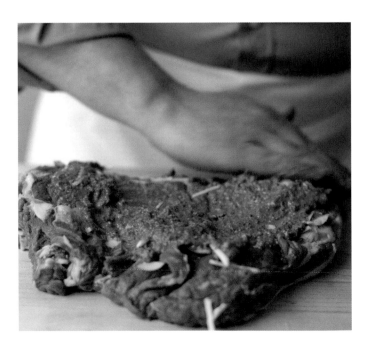

LEFT TO RIGHT Evenly spread the Berbere Paste over the butterflied lamb to ensure that the flavor of the marinade is evenly distributed. The Berbere Grilled Leg of Lamb shown here is served with Grilled Leeks (page 144) and Grilled Potato and Red Onion Fans (page 156).

Berbere Spice Paste

MAKES 2¾ CUPS

4 pequin chiles, seeds and stem removed

2 tsp cardamom seeds

1 tsp coriander seeds

1 tsp cumin seeds

1 tsp fenugreek seeds

1 tsp black peppercorns

¼ tsp allspice berries

¼ tsp whole cloves

1 cup coarsely chopped yellow onion

2 tbsp garlic cloves

2 tbsp Hungarian paprika

1 tbsp cayenne

½ tsp ground ginger

¼ tsp ground cinnamon

¼ tsp grated nutmeg

¼ cup red wine vinegar

¼ cup vegetable oil

1 cup water, as needed

1. Toast the pequin chiles, cardamom seeds, coriander seeds, cumin seeds, fenugreek seeds, black peppercorns (whole), allspice berries, and cloves in a dry skillet until aromatic, 4 minutes. Transfer to a cool bowl and let the spices cool to room temperature.

2. Grind the whole spices and chiles in a food processor until coarsely ground. Add the onion, garlic, paprika, cayenne, ginger, cinnamon, and nutmeg. Process to a coarse, heavy paste.

3. Add the vinegar and oil with the machine running. Add the water gradually, stopping when you have a loose paste.

4. The mixture is ready to use now or it can be transferred to a container and stored in the refrigerator for up to 3 weeks.

Butterflying Meats

When a butterfly opens its wings, it looks doubled in size. The idea behind butterflying a cut of meat is to create an evenly thin cut with lots of surface area from a cut that is not naturally thin and flat in shape.

To butterfly a leg of lamb, unroll a boneless leg roast so that it lies flat, with the smooth side of the meat facing down. The rougher side, the side that was next to the bone, should be facing up.

You'll see that some parts of the roast are thicker than others. Rest your hand over that part of the roast, keeping it parallel to the cutting surface. Holding a boning or filleting knife parallel to the work surface, make a horizontal slice into the meat. The cut should go from the interior toward the outside edge of the roast. Continue cutting just through the thicker portion. Stop cutting about ½ inch away from the edge of the meat to make a hinge.

Open out the meat flat, just the way you would open a book. Press the meat flat. Keep making cuts like this over the surface of the roast until you have a piece that has an even thickness. Pound the meat slightly to be sure that it cooks evenly on the grill.

FISH AND SEAFOOD

FINDING A GREAT source for perfectly fresh fish and sea-food is the grill cook's greatest challenge. Once you've located a reliable source, rely upon them to guide you to other types of fish and seafood you can try in these recipes. Try an unusual appetizer from Southeast Asia, a grilled lobster dinner with Italian inspiration, or a Mexican favorite, fish tacos. Planked salmon comes from the Pacific Northwest and fish kebabs are paired with an Indian-style cilantro and cashew chutney.

Almost any fish can be successfully prepared on the grill, as long as you take the proper steps to protect it from sticking or tearing. Most recipes call for one or more of the following steps:

> *Marinate the fish with an acid like lemon or lime juice, wine, or vinegar; it helps to firm the flesh a little before the fish goes on the grill.*

> *Oil the fish liberally.*

> *Leave the skin on if possible; you can always remove it before eating, but some fish have a delicious skin that gets crisp and crunchy as it grills.*

> *Use a hand rack to hold the fish; as long as you've oiled the rack well, the fish will be easier to handle. Hand racks are hinged so that they can close around the fish. They are perfect for delicate or lean fish.*

Seafood 101

A fish can have a firm, meaty texture or a delicate, flaky one. Its flavor can be mild or robust; often, the fattier the fish, the more pronounced its flavor. The way fish swim, the water they swim in, and their diets all influence the flavor and texture of their flesh. Being familiar with these distinctions is useful when you want to substitute one type of fish for another in a recipe or want to find a recipe for a type of fish that is new to you.

Finfish have gills and fins. They live in oceans, ponds, rivers, and streams. Some species live in saltwater, others in fresh water. Round fish varieties include trout, bass, snapper, tuna, and salmon. The most popular flatfish varieties include flounder, sole, halibut, and turbot. Sharks, skate, monkfish, and ray are cartilaginous fish, meaning they have cartilage instead of bones.

Clams, mussels, oysters, and scallops are all bivalve mollusks, shellfish with two shells joined by a hinge. Clam and oyster varieties often carry the name of the area where they are harvested. Mussel types include standard (or horse) mussels, pen shell, and New Zealand green lipped. The two main types of scallops are sea scallops and bay scallops.

Lobsters, crabs, crayfish, shrimp, and prawns are all crustaceans. They have jointed exterior skeletons or shells. There are both salt- and freshwater crustaceans. The texture of their flesh is affected by the temperature of the water where they are harvested. Squid, octopus, and cuttlefish belong to a group of shellfish known as cephalopods. Instead of an exterior shell or skeleton, they have an interior shell called a quill.

Today, many varieties of seafood, including catfish, trout, salmon, mussels, and oysters, are farmraised. Fish raised on farms are usually of consistent size and quality, although their flavor may be less pronounced than that of "wild" varieties. The jury is still out on the extent of the repercussions farm-raised fish have on the environment and the survival of wild species.

Grilling Temperatures and Times for Fish and Seafood

Times listed are for medium doneness, or 145°F; cook slightly less for meatier fish, like tuna or swordfish, if you prefer medium-rare.

Fish fillets or steaks	½ inch thick	2 to 3 minutes per side, direct high heat
Fish fillets or steaks	1 inch thick	4 to 5 minutes per side, direct high heat
Fish fillets or steaks	1½ inches thick	5 to 6 minutes per side, direct high heat
Whole fish, pan-dressed	1 pound	8 to 10 minutes per side, indirect medium heat
Whole fish, pan-dressed	2 pounds	10 to 12 minutes per side, indirect medium heat
Whole fish, pan-dressed	3 pounds	15 to 18 minutes per side, indirect medium heat
Clams		About 10 minutes over direct high heat, or until clam shells open
Mussels		About 5 minutes over direct high heat, or until mussel shells open
Oysters		About 4 minutes over direct high heat, or until oyster shells open
Lobster	1½ to 2 pounds	10 to 12 minutes per side, indirect medium heat
Scallops		1 to 2 minutes per side, direct high heat
Shrimp		2 to 3 minutes per side, direct high heat

GRILLED SHRIMP PASTE ON SUGARCANE

with Hoisin Peanut Sauce

DON'T LET the long list of ingredients in this recipe put you off. Part of the list includes a table salad, one of the features of a Vietnamese presentation. Unlike many Western salads, a table salad includes plenty of fresh herbs so your guests can flavor their food themselves at the table.

MAKES 8 SERVINGS

2 oz pork fatback

1 tbsp roasted peanut oil

¼ cup minced shallots

12 oz shrimp (31/35 count), peeled, deveined, and chopped

2 tbsp fish sauce

1 tbsp granulated sugar

1 tsp minced garlic

1 large egg

¼ tsp ground white pepper

2 tbsp cornstarch

½ tsp baking powder

¼ cup thinly sliced scallions

16 pieces canned sugarcane (see note below)

8 leaves red-leaf lettuce

1 cup bean sprouts

1 cup European cucumber julienne, skin on

1 tbsp chopped mint

1 tbsp chopped cilantro

1 tbsp chopped Thai basil

3 tbsp Scallion Oil (page 50)

1¼ cups Hoisin Peanut Sauce (page 50)

NOTE: *This recipe calls for canned sugarcane to cut into pieces that you will mold the shrimp paste around. Since the stalks have different sizes, you may need to cut each piece into quarters, sixths, or eighths to make "skewers" that are about ¼ inch thick.*

LEFT TO RIGHT Mold the shrimp paste around the sugarcane using a little bit of pressure so that it adheres to the cane pieces. The shrimp paste should be opaque when it is properly steamed. Grilling the shrimp adds a great deal of flavor; it is important not to grill the shrimp too long or it will become tough and dry.

1. Bring a small pot of water to a boil. Boil the fatback until white and firm, about 10 minutes. Drain and cool the fatback, then mince.

2. Heat the peanut oil in a small pan over medium-high heat. Sweat the shallots in the oil until translucent, about 2 minutes. Transfer the fatback and shallots to a mixing bowl and let cool to room temperature.

3. Add the shrimp, fish sauce, sugar, garlic, egg, pepper, cornstarch, and baking powder to the fatback mixture. Mix well to coat the shrimp evenly with all of the ingredients.

4. Transfer the mixture to the bowl of a food processor. Pulse into a smooth paste, about 30 seconds. (Do not over-mix or the paste will toughen.) Transfer the mixture to a bowl and stir in the scallions.

5. Wet your hands, and form about 2 tbsp of the shrimp paste into a ball. Flatten the paste until it is about ½ inch thick, and place a piece of sugarcane in the center. Wrap the paste around the cane, making the paste about 1 inch thick and leaving about ½ inch of exposed cane on both ends to use for handles. Press the paste onto the cane so it sticks. Lightly oil your hands and smooth the surface. Set aside on an oiled plate. Finish molding all the paste onto the sugar-cane pieces.

6. Preheat a gas grill to medium. If you are using a char-coal grill, build a fire and let it burn down until the coals are glowing red with a moderate coating of white ash. Spread the coals in an even bed. Clean the cooking grate.

7. Set the skewered shrimp paste in a steamer basket lined with lettuce leaves. Set over a pot of simmering water, cover, and steam the shrimp paste on the sugarcane until just cooked through and firm, 3 to 5 minutes. If unsure, break one open and check the middle for doneness and color.

8. Place the steamed shrimp pieces on the grill over direct heat. Grill for 1 minute, then give each piece a quarter turn. Grill for another minute. Flip each piece over and grill for an-other 3 minutes, or until the shrimp is heated through and there are ample grill marks.

9. To make the table salad: Arrange a lettuce leaf, a small pile of bean sprouts, and a small pile of cucumber on each plate. Combine the herbs and sprinkle on top of the bean sprouts and the cucumber. Drizzle the salads with the Scal-lion Oil. Place 2 pieces of the grilled shrimp on top of each salad. Spoon the Hoisin Peanut Sauce over the shrimp pieces. Serve immediately.

Scallion Oil

MAKES 1 CUP

½ cup vegetable oil
½ cup thinly sliced scallions

1. Combine the oil and scallions in a small sauté pan and heat over medium flame until the oil begins to sizzle, about 1 minute.

2. Remove from heat and let cool to room temperature. The oil is ready to use now or it may be stored in the refrigerator for up to 3 days.

Hoisin Peanut Sauce

MAKES 1¼ CUPS

½ cup hoisin sauce
¼ cup water
¼ cup rice vinegar
¼ cup minced shallots
1 tbsp Vietnamese chili-garlic paste
1 tbsp chopped roasted unsalted peanuts

1. Combine the hoisin, water, rice vinegar, and shallots in a small sauté pan and bring to a boil over high heat. Reduce heat to medium and simmer for 5 minutes, until the sauce darkens slightly and lightly coats the back of a spoon.

2. Remove from heat and let cool to room temperature. Stir in the chili-garlic paste and peanuts. The sauce is ready to use now or it may be stored in a container in the refriger-ator for up to 1 week.

FIRECRACKER SHRIMP

W E USED pancetta in this recipe, but feel free to use sliced bacon instead.

MAKES 6 SERVINGS

2 pounds shrimp (16/20 count)

12 bamboo skewers

3 tbsp extra-virgin olive oil

2 tsp grated lemon zest

¼ tsp ground cayenne pepper

2 tsp chopped thyme

2 tbsp chopped flat-leaf parsley

⅓ lb pancetta, sliced as thinly as possible

Juice of 1 lemon

1. Remove the shells from the shrimp, leaving on the part that covers the tails, and devein.

2. Soak the skewers in cool water for about 30 minutes.

3. Combine the olive oil, lemon zest, cayenne, thyme, and 4 tsp of the chopped parsley in a bowl. Add the shrimp and toss to coat all the shrimp evenly. Cover, and marinate in the refrigerator for at least 30 minutes and up to 2 hours.

4. Preheat a gas grill to high. If you are using a charcoal grill, build a fire and let it burn down until the coals are glowing red with a light coating of white ash. Spread the coals in an even bed. Clean the cooking grate.

5. Remove the shrimp from the marinade and let any excess drain off. Wrap a pancetta slice around each shrimp, overlapping the pancetta slightly. Thread the shrimp on the skewers.

6. Cook the shrimp until the pancetta begins to color and the shrimp are cooked through, about 2 minutes per side.

7. Remove the cooked shrimp from the skewers and toss with the lemon juice and the remaining parsley. Serve while still warm.

Peeling and Deveining Shrimp

To peel shrimp, start from the belly side and peel away the legs along with the shell. Pull off the tail if desired, or leave it intact to serve as a handle for shrimp to be eaten with the fingers.

For shrimp that will be presented whole and peeled, you should remove the vein that runs along the back of the shrimp for a cleaner-tasting dish.

To devein shrimp, lay the peeled shrimp on a work surface. With the curved outer edge of the shrimp facing your cutting hand, use a paring knife to make a shallow cut along the shrimp's back. Use the tip of the knife to scrape out the gray or black vein, which is actually the shrimp's intestinal tract.

GRILLED SHRIMP AND PINEAPPLE

with Adobo de Achiote

THE ACHIOTE seeds used to make the marinade for this dish contribute a rich flavor that some describe as earthy as well as a rusty reddish-orange color. This sauce, which combines the achiote seeds with vinegar and spices, is thought to have its origins in the Yucatán Pensisula.

MAKES 8 SERVINGS

16 bamboo skewers

½ cup lime juice

2 tbsp chopped garlic

2 tbsp achiote seeds

4 tsp cider vinegar

2 tsp allspice berries

2 tsp dried Mexican oregano

2 tsp salt

1½ tsp whole black peppercorns

⅔ cup vegetable or olive oil

1 large pineapple

2 medium-sized red onions

2¼ lb shrimp (21/25 count)

2 cups Guacamole (page 35)

2 cups Chipotle Pico de Gallo (page 72)

1. Soak the skewers in cool water for 30 minutes.

2. To make the achiote paste: Place the lime juice, garlic, achiote seeds, vinegar, allspice, oregano, salt, and peppercorns in a blender and purée until smooth. Add the oil with the blender running and continue to blend until the mixture is very smooth. Transfer the mixture to a bowl and set aside, to allow the flavors to blend.

3. Cut the peel off of the pineapple and cut the flesh into ½-inch-thick slices. Core the pineapple slices and cut each slice into 8 wedges. There should be 48 wedges total.

4. Peel the onions and remove the core. Cut each onion into ½-inch-thick slices and cut each slice into 8 wedges. There should be 32 wedges total.

5. Thread each skewer with 3 shrimp, 3 pineapples wedges, and 2 red onion wedges. As you assemble the skewers, transfer them to a shallow pan. Once they are all assembled, pour the achiote paste over them and turn to coat evenly. Marinate in the refrigerator for at least 1 and up to 3 hours.

6. Preheat a gas grill to high. If you are using a charcoal grill, build a fire and let it burn down until the coals are glowing red with a light coating of white ash. Spread the coals in an even bed. Clean the cooking grate.

7. Place the skewers on the grill and cook on both sides until cooked through, about 3 to 4 minutes per side. Serve hot or at room temperature with the Guacamole and Pico de Gallo on the side.

SPICY ASIAN GRILLED SHRIMP

and Marinated Vegetable Salad

THIS DISH adheres to the Asian principle of balancing all of the basic tastes. It is highly perfumed, almost heady, with only a suggestion of heat from the ginger and chili sauce.

MAKES 6 SERVINGS

12 bamboo skewers

2 tbsp rice wine vinegar

2 tbsp minced garlic

1 tbsp minced ginger

1 tbsp chili sauce

1 tbsp Thai fish sauce

2 tsp five-spice powder

2 tsp dark sesame oil

2½ lb shrimp (16/20 count), peeled and deveined

Marinated Vegetable Salad (recipe follows)

1. Soak the skewers in cool water for about 30 minutes.

2. Combine the vinegar, garlic, ginger, chili sauce, fish sauce, five-spice powder, and sesame oil in a bowl. Add the shrimp and toss to coat all the shrimp evenly. Cover, and marinate in the refrigerator for at least 1 and up to 3 hours.

3. Preheat a gas grill to high. If you are using a charcoal grill, build a fire and let it burn down until the coals are glowing red with a light coating of white ash. Spread the coals in an even bed. Clean the cooking grate.

4. Remove the shrimp from the marinade and let any excess drain off. Thread the shrimp onto the skewers.

5. Place the skewers on the grill and cook on both sides until cooked through, about 3 to 4 minutes per side. Serve on a bed of the Marinated Vegetable Salad.

Marinated Vegetable Salad

LOOK FOR unsalted raw nuts at natural food stores. Remember to store any nuts you don't use for this recipe in the freezer, where they'll keep for up to 3 months; raw nuts which are stored at room temperature can quickly become rancid.

MAKES 6 SERVINGS

1½ cups grated carrot

1½ cups grated daikon radish

2 tbsp minced pickled ginger

¼ cup vegetable oil

1 tbsp olive oil

1 tbsp peanut oil

1½ tsp sesame oil

2 tbsp rice wine vinegar

1 tsp soy sauce

1 tsp Thai fish sauce

Pinch ground white pepper

Pinch cayenne pepper

1 tbsp chopped unsalted roasted peanuts

1½ tsp toasted sesame seeds

Toss together the carrot, daikon radish, and ginger in a bowl. Combine the remaining ingredients in a separate bowl and mix well. Pour over the carrot mixture, and toss to mix. Cover and refrigerate until ready to serve.

GRILLED BABY OCTOPUS

with Coconut Rice

BRAISING THE octopus gently before you grill it gives it a unique texture. You can save the braising liquid to use as the base for a seafood soup or stew.

MAKES 8 SERVINGS

OCTOPUS

2 tbsp olive oil

½ cup medium-dice yellow onion

½ cup medium-dice carrot

¼ cup medium-dice celery

1½ tsp minced garlic

2 lb baby octopus

½ cup dry white wine

1½ cups water

1 cup tomato juice

4 thyme sprigs

2 rosemary sprigs

2 bay leaves

1 tsp salt

1 tsp ground black pepper

MARINADE

½ cup olive oil

¼ cup thyme leaves

¼ cup thinly sliced scallions

1 tbsp minced garlic

Salt, to taste

Ground black pepper, to taste

Coconut Rice (page 57)

1. To prepare the octopus: Heat the olive oil in a saucepot over medium heat. Add the onion, carrot, and celery, and sweat, stirring occasionally, until tender and translucent, about 8 minutes. Add the garlic and sweat until aromatic, about 1 minute. Add the octopus and continue to cook, turning, until the octopus is stiff on all sides, about 5 minutes.

2. Add the white wine to deglaze the pan, and continue to simmer until the wine has reduced to ⅓ its original volume. Add the water, tomato juice, thyme, rosemary, bay leaves, salt, and pepper. Braise the octopus over very low heat, uncovered, until tender, about 1 hour. Remove and discard the bay leaf and herb sprigs. Set aside the octopus in the braising liquid to cool until ready to grill.

3. To make the marinade: Combine the oil, thyme, scallions, and garlic. Add salt and pepper to taste. Set aside.

4. Preheat a gas grill to high. If you are using a charcoal grill, build a fire and let it burn down until the coals are glowing red with a light coating of white ash. Spread the coals in an even bed. Clean the cooking grate.

5. Remove the octopus from the braising liquid and drain well. Brush or roll the octopus in the marinade and grill until marked and very hot, about 2 to 3 minutes per side. Serve the octopus immediately with the Coconut Rice.

GRILLED LOBSTER

with Broccoli Raab & Cannellini Beans with Pancetta

THIS IS an incredible meal. It has a really good ratio of lobster to beans to greens, and the flavor is phenomenal. It is rich and earthy and hearty without being too filling. Peeling all of the lobsters is a little time-consuming for the cook but well worth the effort, since the juices from the lobster work their way into the broccoli raab dish for even more flavor.

MAKES 8 SERVINGS

Water, as needed

Salt, as needed

8 lobsters, about 1½ lb each, prepared for grilling (see below)

2 tbsp olive oil

1 tsp ground black pepper

Broccoli Raab & Cannellini Beans with Pancetta (opposite)

½ cup grated Parmesan

1. Preheat a gas grill to high. If you are using a charcoal grill, build a fire and let it burn down until the coals are glowing red with a light coating of white ash. Spread the coals in an even bed. Clean the cooking grate.

2. Brush the tail and claw meat with the olive oil and season with salt and pepper.

3. Place the prepared lobsters on the grill, shell-side down. Grill the lobsters about 2 to 3 minutes on each side, until the shell turns reddish-orange.

4. Remove the tail and the claw meat from the shells, and cut each tail into ½-inch-thick-slices. Set aside.

5. Divide the Broccoli Raab & Cannellini Beans with Pancetta among 8 serving plates and sprinkle with the Parmesan cheese. Place the tail and claw meat of each lobster atop the broccoli raab and bean mixture and serve.

Preparing Lobster for the Grill

Purchasing live lobster for cooking guarantees the best flavor and texture. Lay a live lobster belly-side down on a work surface, head pointing toward your cutting hand. Insert the tip of a chef's knife into the base of its head to kill the lobster quickly, and pull the knife all the way down through the shell, splitting the head in half. Turn the lobster 180 degrees. Place the tip of the knife at the same point as your first cut, and then cut completely through the shell of the body and tail.

REMOVING THE MEAT FROM A COOKED LOBSTER

If a recipe calls for only the meat of a cooked lobster, you will need to partially cook the lobster by either grilling, broiling, boiling, or steam-ing it just until the shell turns a bright color. This firms up the flesh enough so that it will separate from the shell. If you try to pull the flesh from a raw lobster, you will simply pull apart the flesh. Once the lobster is partially cooked, let it cool completely. Twist the tail away from the body. Squeeze the underside of the tail shell to crack it partially and loosen it, then pull the tail meat away in one piece.

Stand the claw on the work surface with its "thumb" edge down. Use the heel of the knife to cut into the outside edge of each claw, without cutting through to the meat, then swivel the knife sharply to the side to crack apart the claw shell. Remove the claw in one piece by wiggling the meat as you pull it out, taking care to slip the "thumb" out slowly. Use a large knife or kitchen shears to cut through the leg knuckles, then pull out the knuckle meat.

Broccoli Raab & Cannellini Beans with Pancetta

MAKES 8 SERVINGS

2 tbsp olive oil

¼ cup diced pancetta or bacon

½ cup minced yellow onion

2 tsp minced garlic

2 bunches broccoli raab, trimmed

2 cups cooked or canned cannellini beans, drained and rinsed

½ cup chicken or vegetable broth

1 tsp salt

½ tsp ground black pepper

1. Heat the olive oil in a large sauté pan over medium heat. Add the pancetta or bacon and sauté until the fat renders and the pancetta is translucent, about 1 minute.

2. Add the onion and sauté, stirring frequently, until golden brown, about 5 to 6 minutes. Add the garlic and continue to sauté until the garlic is aromatic, about 1 minute more.

3. Add the broccoli raab by handfuls, stirring and sautéing until the leaves just wilt before adding more. Add the cannellini beans and the broth.

4. Bring to a simmer and cook until the broccoli raab is bright green and tender, about 3 to 4 minutes. Season the mixture with salt and pepper. Keep warm until ready to serve.

Coconut Rice

MAKES 8 SERVINGS

¼ cup butter

1 tbsp minced garlic

2 tbsp minced ginger

3 cups long-grain white rice

2 cups coconut milk

4 cups water

1 tsp salt

½ tsp ground black pepper

1 cup golden raisins

1 cup toasted, sliced almonds

1. Heat the butter in a saucepan. Add the garlic and ginger, and sauté until fragrant, about 2 minutes. Add the rice and sauté until the grains are coated with the butter and give off a toasted aroma.

2. Add the coconut milk, water, salt, and pepper. Bring to a boil, reduce to a light simmer, and cover. Cook until the rice is tender, about 18 minutes.

3. Fluff the rice with a fork, add the raisins and almonds, and toss lightly to mix. Keep warm, covered, until ready to use.

SEAFOOD GRILL

with Tamarind Glaze

THE TROPICAL tamarind tree is valued for its plump, dark brown pods, which are filled with a sticky, stringy pulp peppered with large seeds. Tart and refreshing, with a more complex astringency than that of citrus, tamarind pulp is used extensively in Indian and Southeast Asian cooking. Look for jars of tamarind concentrate in Indian or Asian groceries.

MAKES 8 SERVINGS

1 cup tamarind concentrate

1 cup olive oil

½ cup white vinegar

½ cup fresh lime juice

¼ cup honey

2 tbsp Dijon mustard

8 scallions, minced

¼ cup minced basil

2 tbsp minced garlic

2 tbsp toasted cumin seeds

1 tsp red pepper flakes

2 lb sea bass or yellowtail fillets, cut into 2-inch cubes

2 lb jumbo shrimp, peeled and deveined, tails on

2 lb sea scallops

16 bamboo skewers

24 littleneck clams

1. Whisk together the tamarind, olive oil, vinegar, lime juice, honey, mustard, scallions, basil, garlic, cumin seeds, and red pepper flakes in a baking dish to make a marinade. Reserve 1 cup to use as a dipping sauce.

2. Add the sea bass, shrimp, and scallops to the dish, and turn to coat all the seafood evenly. Cover, and refrigerate for at least 30 minutes or up to 2 hours.

3. Soak the skewers in cool water for 30 minutes to prevent them from scorching.

4. Preheat a gas grill to high. If you are using a charcoal grill, build a fire and let it burn down until the coals are glowing red with a light coating of white ash. Spread the coals in an even bed. Clean the cooking grate.

5. Remove the seafood from the marinade and let the excess drain off. Thread the shrimp and scallops alternately onto 8 of the skewers. Thread the pieces of sea bass on the remaining skewers.

6. Place the skewers and the clams on the grill. Grill the shrimp and scallops until the scallops are barely opaque and the shrimp are pink, turning once or as needed to mark them evenly on all sides, about 2 to 3 minutes total. Grill the clams until they open, 5 to 6 minutes, being careful to reserve their juices when removing them from the grill. Discard any that do not open. Grill the sea bass skewers on the first side until marked. Gently turn the fish over and continue cooking until barely opaque, 5 to 6 minutes.

7. Serve the grilled seafood with the reserved tamarind dipping sauce.

SHORE DINNER

W E'VE SUBSTITUTED a steamer on the grill here, but kept the seaweed from the classic shore dinner. It adds a special briny savor, but if you can't find it, substitute lettuce leaves or simply omit altogether.

MAKES 8 SERVINGS

¼ cup unsalted butter

2 cups finely chopped yellow onions

2 tsp minced garlic

4 cups chicken broth

2 cups water

4 thyme sprigs

4 small bay leaves

4 handfuls fresh seaweed

4 lobsters, 1¼ lb each

32 littleneck clams, scrubbed

4 small zucchini, halved lengthwise and cut into quarters

24 red bliss potatoes, par-cooked

4 ears corn, shucked and halved crosswise

4 leeks, split lengthwise

1½ lb cod fillet, cut into 8 pieces

20 mussels, scrubbed and debearded

8 sea scallops

¼ cup chopped flat-leaf parsley

Lemon wedges, for garnish

¾ cup drawn butter

1. Preheat a gas grill to medium heat. If you are using a charcoal grill, build a fire and let it burn down until the coals are glowing red with a moderate coating of white ash. Spread the coals in an even bed. Clean the cooking grate.

2. Melt the unsalted butter in the bottom of the steamer over the grill. Add the onions and garlic, and cook until aromatic. Add the broth, water, thyme, and bay leaves, and bring to a boil.

3. Make a bed of seaweed on the bottom of the steaming basket. Kill the lobsters by making a small incision in the back of the shell where the chest and tail meet. Place the lobsters on top of the seaweed and top them with the clams, zucchini, and potatoes. Place the basket over the boiling broth. Cover the steamer and cook for 5 to 8 minutes.

4. While the first tier is cooking, arrange the corn, leeks, cod, mussels, and scallops on the steamer's second tier. Add the second tier to the steamer, cover, and continue to steam for another 5 minutes, or until the clams and mussels are open; the lobsters, cod, and scallops are opaque throughout; and the vegetables are tender.

5. Remove the lobsters from the steamer and split in half. Remove all the other food and arrange it in warmed casseroles or serving bowls. Sprinkle with chopped parsley and moisten with the broth. Serve with the lemon wedges and melted butter.

Shore Dinners

A shore dinner is traditionally cooked in a pit that has been dug in the sand near the ocean. The hole is filled with driftwood that is set on fire. After the fire is established, rocks are added to the pit to absorb the heat. Finally, a layer of seaweed is set over the rocks as a bed onto which the various ingredients are added: lobsters, clams, mussels, oysters, potatoes, corn, leeks, and zucchini. Then, another layer of seaweed, and finally, a heavy tarp over the pit to trap the heat and steam.

CEDAR-PLANKED SALMON

with Huckleberry-Zinfandel Sauce

THE WOOD adds a lot of flavor to fish as you cook it. For variety, you can use hickory, mesquite, or even fruit tree wood, like apple or cherry. The planks don't last forever, but you should be able to get more than one cooking session from them. You may be able to find smaller, thinner planks that are perfect for individual servings. The sauce we suggest here is a classic brown sauce finished with wild huckleberries. If you want something a little simpler, try one of the compound butters on pages 117–119 or the Scallion Oil on page 50.

MAKES 8 SERVINGS

3 lb salmon fillet

1 tbsp salt

1 tsp ground black pepper

2 cedar planks, soaked overnight

2 cups Zinfandel Sauce (recipe follows)

1 cup huckleberries

1. Preheat a gas grill to medium-high heat. If you are using a charcoal grill, build a fire and let it burn down until the coals are glowing red with a light coating of white ash. Spread the coals in an even bed. Clean the cooking grate.

2. Clean, dry, and trim the salmon to remove any remaining belly bones or pin bones. Cut the salmon into 8 equal pieces and then season with the salt and pepper.

3. Place 4 salmon fillets on each soaked cedar plank, and place the planks on the grill. Grill, covered, until just cooked through, about 8 to 10 minutes.

4. Combine the Zinfandel Sauce with the huckleberries.

5. Serve the salmon with ¼ cup of sauce per portion. Garnish with the huckleberries, if desired.

Zinfandel Sauce

THIS IS one instance when making your own broth from rich meaty beef or veal bones that you've roasted

LEFT TO RIGHT Grill the salmon until it is just cooked through; the plank should be slightly charred. Be sure to take the time to reduce the sauce properly; the velvety texture and rich flavor will reward your patience. Opposite, the Cedar-Planked Salmon with Huckleberry-Zinfandel Sauce is served here with Grilled Belgian Endive (page 133).

beforehand makes a world of difference. Most canned broths are too salty once you've reduced them to a sauce consistency. The quality of the wine is paramount to the flavor of the sauce, too, so don't skimp.

1 tbsp vegetable oil

½ cup medium-dice carrot

½ cup medium-dice yellow onion

¼ cup medium-dice celery

1 tbsp tomato paste

1½ cups Zinfandel wine

8 cups beef broth

1 bay leaf

6 parsley stems

1 thyme sprig

1 garlic clove, peeled and left whole

Salt, to taste

Ground black pepper, to taste

1. Heat the oil in a large stockpot over medium-high heat. Add the carrots and onions and sauté until the onions are golden brown, 10 to 12 minutes. Add the celery and continue to sauté until the celery is tender, another 8 minutes.

2. Immediately stir in the tomato paste and cook until the mixture takes on a rust color, about 4 minutes.

3. Deglaze the pan with the wine, and simmer until reduced by half.

4. Add the broth, bay leaf, parsley stems, thyme, and garlic, and simmer until the sauce is just thick enough to lightly coat the back of a spoon. Add salt and pepper to taste. Keep warm until ready to use.

Filleting a Round Fish

A filleting or boning knife with a flexible blade is ideal for the delicate work of filleting fish. Place the fish on a work surface with its back toward you. Make a cut behind the head and gills down to the bone, angling the knife away from the body, but do not sever the head.

CUTTING THE FIRST FILLET

Without lifting the knife, angle it so that the blade is parallel to the work surface and the cutting edge is pointing toward the fish's tail. Hold the knife handle lower than the blade, to remove as much flesh from the bone as possible. Run the knife down the length of the fish, under the flesh, to cut a fillet. Press the knife against the bones as you slice and do not saw back and forth. Remove the fillet from the bones and place skin-side down.

REMOVING THE BACKBONE

Without turning the fish over, insert the blade just underneath the backbone. Lay your guiding hand flat on top of the bone structure to keep the fish stable. Keeping the knife parallel to the work surface, run the blade down the entire length of the fish underneath the bones. The knife's cutting edge should be angled upward very slightly to cut as much flesh from bone as possible.

TRIMMING THE FILLETS

Remove the belly bones by making smooth strokes against the bones to cut them away cleanly. Trim away excess fat only on the belly edge of the fillets. Cut away the remnants of the backbone by running the blade just underneath the line of the backbone, lifting it up and away from the fillet as you cut.

REMOVING THE PIN BONES

As you look at the fillet, you'll see a midline running its length. To locate the pin bones, run a fingertip down the length of the fillets to one side of the midline. Use tweezers or needlenose pliers to pull the pin bones out, working with the grain to avoid tearing the flesh.

SALMON BLT

THIS VARIATION of a classic BLT pairs grilled salmon with a rich sauce punctuated with briny, salty capers. If you have the grill on the night before, you can grill the salmon ahead of time, but be certain you chill the fish quickly and keep it in the refrigerator until you are ready to assemble the sandwiches. Choose bread that is firm enough to hold up to toasting. Rye is a great choice with salmon.

MAKES 8 SERVINGS

1 cup mayonnaise

2¼ tsp chopped capers

Salt, to taste

Ground black pepper, to taste

¼ cup olive oil

2 lb salmon fillet

16 slices bread (whole wheat, rye, or peasant style), toasted

16 leaves green leaf lettuce

24 strips bacon, cooked until crisp

24 slices tomato (about 4 beefsteak tomatoes)

1. Preheat a gas grill to high. If you are using a charcoal grill, build a fire and let it burn down until the coals are glowing red with a light coating of white ash. Spread the coals in an even bed. Clean the cooking grate.

2. Stir together the mayonnaise and capers. Season with salt and pepper.

3. Season the oil generously with salt and pepper.

4. Cut the salmon into 8 equal pieces. Brush the salmon pieces with the seasoned oil. Grill the salmon until cooked through, about 2 minutes on each side.

5. Spread the caper mayonnaise on the toasted bread. Place 1 lettuce leaf and 1 piece grilled salmon on a slice of toast. Layer it with a second lettuce leaf, 3 bacon strips, and 3 tomato slices. Top with a slice of toast. Secure the sandwich with long toothpicks and cut in half. Assemble the remaining sandwiches in the same manner.

SMOKED SALMON

ALTHOUGH IMPORTED smoked salmon carries a distinct cachet, there are many advantages to producing your own. With experience you can learn to control the subtleties and create a signature smoked salmon that simply can't be found in a store.

MAKES 12 SERVINGS

1 salmon fillet, skin on, about 3 lb

1½ cups salt

½ cup granulated sugar

2 tsp onion powder

¾ tsp ground cloves

¾ tsp ground or crushed bay leaf

¾ tsp ground mace

¾ tsp ground allspice

1. Remove the pin bones from the salmon and center it skin-side down on a large piece of cheesecloth.

2. Mix together the remaining ingredients thoroughly and pack evenly over the salmon. (The layer should be slightly thinner where the fillet tapers to the tail.)

3. Wrap the salmon loosely in the cheesecloth and place it on a rack in a pan. Cure the salmon in the refrigerator for at least 12 and up to 24 hours.

4. Gently rinse off the cure with cool water and blot dry. Air-dry uncovered on a rack in the refrigerator overnight to form a dry skin.

5. Preheat a smoker to 225° to 250° F following the manufacturer's instructions. Place the salmon on a rack in the smoker, cover, and smoke until the salmon is firm to the touch and has a rich golden color, about 2 hours.

PESCE SPADA SICILIANA

(Grilled Swordfish Sicilian-Style)

THE SWORDFISH in this recipe could easily be replaced with halibut or sea bass. You want to use a meaty, firm fish that will hold up well when grilled.

MAKES 6 SERVINGS

½ cup olive oil

Juice of 2 lemons

3 tbsp chopped capers

3 tbsp chopped oregano

6 swordfish steaks, 6 oz each

3 cups Siciliana Sauce (recipe follows)

½ cup sliced almonds, toasted

Couscous with Almonds and Raisins (page 66)

1. Combine the olive oil, lemon juice, capers, and oregano to make a marinade. Clean and dry the steaks. Place the swordfish steaks in a shallow pan and pour the marinade over them. Turn the steaks to coat them evenly. Let marinate in the refrigerator for at least 30 minutes and up to 2 hours.

2. Preheat a gas grill to high. If you are using a charcoal grill, build a fire and let it burn down until the coals are glowing red with a light coating of white ash. Spread the coals in an even bed. Clean the cooking grate.

3. Grill the swordfish for about 4 minutes per side, or until cooked through. Transfer to a warm platter, top with the Siciliana Sauce, and garnish with the sliced almonds. Serve on a bed of the Couscous with Almonds and Raisins.

Sicililana Sauce

MAKES 3 CUPS

IF YOU can't find olives stuffed with chiles at your local grocer, check at an Italian deli; they may have freshly stuffed olives. This sauce also goes well with chicken or veal.

⅓ cup olive oil

1 cup minced yellow onion

3 tbsp chopped capers

6 anchovy fillets

1 tbsp minced garlic

3 pints cherry tomatoes, hulled

½ cup olives stuffed with chiles

3 tbsp chopped oregano

½ tsp salt

¼ tsp black pepper

1. Heat the olive oil in a skillet over medium heat. Add the onions, capers, anchovy fillets, and garlic; sauté, stirring frequently, until the onions are a very light golden brown, about 8 to 10 minutes.

2. Add the tomatoes and continue to sauté, tossing frequently, until the tomatoes are very soft, about 10 minutes.

3. Add the olives, oregano, salt, and pepper; sauté for another 2 to 3 minutes. Adjust seasonings to taste with salt and pepper if necessary. Keep warm until ready to use.

The Pesce Spada Siciliana is served on a bed of the couscous along with Grilled Artichokes with Hazlenut Romesco Sauce (page 124).

Couscous with Almonds and Raisins

MAKES 6 SERVINGS

1 cup raisins

 2 cups boiling water

3 cups chicken broth

2 tbsp olive oil

1 tbsp salt

1½ tsp ground black pepper

2 cups couscous

1 cup toasted almonds or pine nuts

¼ cup chopped parsley

3 tbsp extra-virgin olive oil

1. Place the raisins in a small bowl and add enough boiling water to cover them. Let the raisins sit in the water until they plump and soften, about 5 to 7 minutes.

2. Bring the chicken broth to a boil in a large saucepan and add the olive oil, salt, and pepper.

3. Stir in the couscous, making sure that all of it is wet. Cover and set the saucepan aside in a warm place until the couscous is tender, 15 to 20 minutes.

4. Stir in the raisins, toasted almonds or pine nuts, and parsley. Drizzle the extra-virgin olive oil over the top.

GRILLED MARINATED SWORDFISH SKEWERS

THIS GREEK-INSPIRED skewer of swordfish features a healthy amount of garlic. Be sure to slice it just before making the marinade for the best flavor.

MAKES 8 SERVINGS

1 cup lemon juice

3 tbsp sliced garlic

⅔ cup extra-virgin olive oil

1 tbsp dried oregano

3½ lb swordfish, boneless and skinless, cut into 1¼-inch cubes

16 bamboo skewers

1 tsp salt

1. Combine the lemon juice, garlic, extra-virgin olive oil, and oregano to make a marinade. Add the swordfish to the marinade and stir gently to coat. Let marinate in the refrigerator for 30 minutes.

2. Soak the skewers in cool water for 30 minutes.

3. Preheat a gas grill to medium-high. If you are using a charcoal grill, build a fire and let it burn down until the coals are glowing red with a moderate coating of white ash. Spread the coals in an even bed. Clean the cooking grate.

4. Wipe excess marinade from the swordfish and thread onto the skewers. Season to taste with salt. Grill the swordfish until the flesh is opaque and firm, about 4 minutes per side. Serve immediately.

FISH KEBABS

with Cilantro and Cashew Chutney

THIS IS a magnificent dish. The fish picks up a lot of flavor from the marinade, which also makes it very tender. The Cilantro and Cashew Chutney packs an incredible burst of flavor and texture.

MAKES 8 SERVINGS

1 cup whole-milk yogurt

½ cup peanut butter

1 jalapeño, minced

1 tbsp thyme leaves

1 tbsp ground fennel seeds

1 tbsp ground white pepper

½ tsp salt

3 tbsp lemon juice

1 tbsp minced ginger

2 tsp minced garlic

3 lb mahi-mahi or swordfish, cut into 1-inch cubes

16 bamboo skewers

1½ cups Cilantro and Cashew Chutney (recipe follows)

1. Mix together the yogurt, peanut butter, jalapeño, thyme, fennel, pepper, salt, 2 tbsp of the lemon juice, the ginger, and garlic in a bowl to make a marinade.

2. Rinse the fish and dry the cubes well with a paper towel. Sprinkle the remaining lemon juice over the fish cubes and let stand for 15 minutes. Remove any excess moisture and place them in the marinade. Refrigerate for at least 1 hour and up to 12 hours.

3. Soak the skewers in cool water for 30 minutes.

4. Preheat a gas grill to medium-high. If you are using a charcoal grill, build a fire and let it burn down until the coals are glowing red with a moderate coating of white ash. Spread the coals in an even bed. Clean the cooking grate.

5. Remove the fish from marinade and thread onto the skewers. Grill the kebabs until cooked through, about 2 minutes per side (8 minutes total). Serve with the Cilantro and Cashew Chutney.

Cilantro and Cashew Chutney

MAKES 1½ CUPS

1 bunch cilantro, stems removed

½ cup unsalted cashews

1 tbsp lemon juice

½ tsp ground cumin

1 jalapeño, halved, seeds and stem removed

1 tsp salt

1 tsp pepper

¾ cup whole-milk yogurt, or more as needed

Combine all the ingredients in a blender and purée until smooth. Add more yogurt if necessary to facilitate blending. Adjust the seasoning to taste with salt and pepper. Refrigerate the chutney until needed.

GRILLED MACKEREL WITH THYME

MACKEREL IS a moderately fatty fish with a distinct flavor. It picks up hints of smokiness from the grill readily, so we've kept seasonings simple here to let the fish shine.

MAKES 6 SERVINGS

2 tbsp lemon juice

4 tsp salt

2 tsp ground black pepper

⅓ cup vegetable oil

12 thyme sprigs

6 pan-dressed Spanish mackerel, 14 oz each

1 lemon, cut into wedges

Grilled Asparagus and Sweet Peppers (page 123)

1. Preheat a gas grill to medium. If you are using a charcoal grill, build a fire and let it burn down until the coals are glowing red with a moderate coating of white ash. Spread the coals in an even bed. Clean the cooking grate.

2. Combine the lemon juice, salt, pepper, and 1 tbsp of the oil. Place 2 thyme sprigs in the cavity of each fish. Brush the lemon juice mixture over the inside and outside of each fish. Brush the outside of the fish with some of the remaining oil. (Reserve any excess oil to brush the fish as it grills if needed.)

3. Grill the fish over direct heat, turning as necessary, until cooked through, about 6 to 8 minutes per side.

4. Serve the mackerel at once on a heated platter or individual plates with the lemon wedges and the Grilled Asparagus and Sweet Peppers.

Serving Oily-fleshed Fish

Fish like mackerel, tuna, herring, sardines, and salmon have a rich texture, due in large part to the oils they contain. Oily fish is a great source for a beneficial type of oil, known as omega-3. You shouldn't shy away from these fish. As long as you keep your servings moderate, most adults can safely enjoy a meal or two each week that features salmon or other oily fish without worry.

When you grill these luscious fish, you have plenty of options when it comes to a good wine to serve. Both white and red wines can be great partners. If you are interested in a white wine, look for wines that are high in acid. Some suggestions include sauvignon blanc, especially those from the Loire Valley in France and from New Zealand. Grüner Veltliner and Rieslings from Austria and Germany are a great match for the rich flavors and textures of these fish. You might also try a white Bordeaux or a crisp rosé from France. The deep flavors from the grill may inspire you to try a red wine with your fish such as Pinot Noir or Beaujolais.

GRILLED BLUEFISH

with Creole Mustard Sauce

OTHER FISH, including salmon, snapper, grouper, or kingfish would all be good substitutes for the bluefish in this recipe. Or ask your fishmonger to suggest a meaty, moderately oily fish. You need a flavorful fish to stand up to the mustard sauce.

MAKES 8 SERVINGS

3 lb bluefish steaks, 6 oz each

Vegetable oil, as needed

Salt, to taste

Ground black pepper, to taste

2 cups Creole Mustard Sauce (recipe follows)

1. Preheat a gas grill to medium-high. If you are using a charcoal grill, build a fire and let it burn down until the coals are glowing red with a moderate coating of white ash. Spread the coals in an even bed. Clean the cooking grate.

2. Brush the fish with the oil and season with salt and pepper. Allow any excess to drain away before placing the fish in a hand rack.

3. Place the hand rack on the grill. Grill undisturbed for about 2 minutes. Turn the fish over and cook until the flesh is opaque and firm, about 2 to 4 minutes more.

4. Serve at once with the Creole Mustard Sauce.

Creole Mustard Sauce

THIS SAUCE features three different kinds of mustard for a complex flavor, but if you don't have all three mustards in your cupboard, feel free to substitute whatever type of good mustard you have on hand.

MAKES 2 CUPS

1 tbsp minced shallots

½ cup cider vinegar

1½ tsp cracked black peppercorns

1 bay leaf

1½ cups dry white wine

½ cup reduced heavy cream (see below)

1¼ lb butter, softened

1 tbsp Dijon mustard

1 tbsp Creole mustard

1 tbsp mild mustard

1. Combine the shallots, vinegar, peppercorns, bay leaf, and wine in a small saucepan over medium-high heat. Reduce the mixture to ½ cup.

2. Add the heavy cream and reduce the mixture by half. Strain the sauce through a fine-mesh sieve and return it to the heat.

3. Whisk in the butter gradually over low heat. Stir in the mustards. Keep warm until needed.

Reducing Heavy Cream

Reduced heavy cream has a thick consistency and a deeper yellow than cream straight from the carton. To reduce heavy cream, pour the cream into a heavy-bottomed saucepan and bring to a simmer over medium heat. Turn the heat down as soon as the cream reaches a simmer to keep it from boiling over. Continue simmering until the cream is reduced to half its original volume.

BAJA-STYLE FISH TACOS

with Southwestern Slaw

PUT THE ingredients for this classic fish taco out on the table and let your family and friends build their own. The combination of fish and coleslaw is heady and robust, a perfect match to the rich taste of the pico de gallo and the lime-scented Mexican crema. If you cannot find Mexican sour cream at the store, substitute regular sour cream. Mexican sour cream has a milder acidic bite and a little more salt.

MAKES 8 SERVINGS

2 lb mahi-mahi

½ cup vegetable oil

3 tbsp lime juice

5 tsp chili powder

1½ tsp ground cumin

1½ tsp ground coriander

1½ tsp minced garlic

Salt, to taste

8 flour tortillas, 8 inches in diameter

Southwestern Slaw (recipe follows)

1 cup Chipotle Pico de Gallo (recipe follows)

½ cup Mexican Crema (recipe follows)

1. Preheat a gas grill to medium-high. If you are using a charcoal grill, build a fire and let it burn down until the coals are glowing red with a moderate coating of white ash. Spread the coals in an even bed. Clean the cooking grate.

2. Cut the mahi-mahi into 16 equal slices.

3. Combine the oil, lime juice, chili powder, cumin, coriander, garlic, and salt. Coat the mahi-mahi with the marinade.

4. Grill the fish on the first side over direct heat until the flesh is firm and well marked, about 2 minutes. Turn the fish and grill until cooked through, about 1½ to 2 minutes more.

5. Grill the tortillas until they have light grill marks and are heated through, about 15 seconds on the first side. Turn the tortillas and grill them until they just start to bubble, another 15 seconds.

6. Center 2 pieces of grilled fish on each tortilla, and top with the Southwestern Slaw and Chipotle Pico de Gallo. Add a dollop of Mexican Crema, fold in half, and serve immediately.

Set up platters of the soft fish tacos so that guests can help themselves or allow them to make their own tacos by putting together a buffet near the grill. The second option cuts down on your assembly time and allows more time for you to enjoy yourself.

Southwestern Slaw

MAKES 8 SERVINGS

2 cups fine-shredded green cabbage

2 tsp lime juice

2 tsp honey

2 tbsp minced red onion

2 tsp minced jalapeños

2 tsp chopped cilantro

Salt, to taste

Combine all the ingredients. Allow the mixture to marinate for at least 30 minutes and up to 8 hours before serving.

Chipotle Pico de Gallo

MAKES 1 CUP

1 cup medium-dice tomatoes (seeded before dicing)

4 tsp minced red onion

½ tsp red wine vinegar

½ canned chipotle pepper, minced

Salt, to taste

1 tbsp cilantro chiffonade

Combine all the ingredients and mix well. The pico de gallo is ready to use now or it can be stored in a covered container in the refrigerator for up to 2 days.

Mexican Crema

MAKES ½ CUP

½ cup Mexican sour cream

½ tsp finely grated lime zest

2 tsp lime juice

Combine all the ingredients and mix well. The cream is ready to use now or it can be stored in a covered container in the refrigerator for up to 2 days.

GRILLED MAHI-MAHI

with Pineapple Chutney

MAHI-MAHI HAS a relatively firm texture, so you could substitute any meaty fish here: halibut, sea bass, tuna, or swordfish.

MAKES 8 SERVINGS

8 mahi-mahi fillets, about 8 oz each

Salt, to taste

Ground black pepper, to taste

Juice of 1 lemon

Vegetable oil, as needed

2½ cups Pineapple Chutney (recipe follows)

1. Preheat a gas grill to medium-high. If you are using a charcoal grill, build a fire and let it burn down until the coals are glowing red with a moderate coating of white ash. Spread the coals in an even bed. Clean the cooking grate.

2. Season the mahi-mahi with salt and pepper and drizzle with the lemon juice. Brush evenly with the oil.

3. Grill the mahi-mahi until marked on one side, about 3 to 4 minutes. Turn the fish over and grill until the fish is cooked through, about 2 minutes more.

4. Serve at once on heated plates with Pineapple Chutney.

Pineapple Chutney

THIS CHUTNEY is best after the flavor has mellowed for about 1 hour and should be enjoyed within 2 days of being made.

MAKES 2½ CUPS

2 cups diced pineapple

¼ cup minced scallions

¼ cup minced cilantro

¼ cup minced red pepper

4 tsp fresh lime juice

Salt, to taste

Ground black pepper, to taste

Ground cayenne pepper, to taste

Toss together the pineapple, scallion, cilantro, and red pepper in a bowl. Season with the lime juice, salt, black pepper, and cayenne to taste. Cover and refrigerate at least 1 hour and up to 2 days before serving.

SMOKED TROUT

with Apple-Horseradish Cream

WHEN YOU apply the salt mixture, make it slightly heavier over the thickest portion of the fish and thinner where the fish begins to taper at the tail. The drying stage, where the fish is left uncovered in the refrigerator, develops a skin that picks up a lot of the smoky flavor. Garde-manger chefs refer to this stage as "forming a pellicle."

MAKES 6 SERVINGS

6 pan-dressed trout, 10 oz each

1 cup kosher salt

½ cup granulated sugar

1 tbsp garlic powder

1 tsp onion powder

1 tsp ground black pepper

Zest of 2 lemons

2 cups mixed baby greens

⅔ cup Lemon Vinaigrette (page 76)

2 Granny Smith apples, thinly sliced

1 cup Apple-Horseradish Cream (page 76)

1. Lay the trout on a baking sheet skin-side up. Scrape the skin lightly with the back side of a knife to remove the scales.

2. Combine the salt, sugar, garlic and onion powders, pepper, and lemon zest.

3. Cover the belly and tail sections of the trout with a ¹⁄₁₆-inch layer of the salt mixture and cover the thicker sections with a ¼-inch layer. Let the trout sit for 30 minutes in the refrigerator. *(recipe continues on page 76)*

LEFT TO RIGHT When placing the fish on the rack to form a pellicle, be sure not to crowd them; they need plenty of air to circulate around them so that they dry evenly. Place the trout skin-side down on the rack that is set over the smoking wood chips; it is important that the wood chips start smoking before adding the trout so that they will get the proper amount of flavor during the time they are in the smoker. Carefully pull the pin bones out with a pair of fish tweezers; this may take a couple of tries, but your guests will appreciate it.

4. Rinse the trout in cold water and place on a wire rack. Let dry, uncovered, in the refrigerator for at least 6 and up to 12 hours.

5. Prepare a smoker according to the manufacturer's instructions or set up a disposable smoker as described below. Place the trout skin-side down in the smoker and let it smoke for 10 to 15 minutes at between 225° and 250°F. If you are using a disposable smoker, the cooking time is about 5 minutes. Remove from the heat and let cool.

6. Toss the greens with the Lemon Vinaigrette. Serve the trout with the dressed greens, sliced apples, and the Apple-Horseradish Cream.

Apple-Horseradish Cream

MAKES 1 CUP

¼ cup heavy cream

¼ cup sour cream

¼ cup grated Granny Smith apple (peeled before grating)

2 tbsp prepared horseradish

¼ tsp salt

1. Whisk the heavy cream until medium-stiff peaks form. Fold in the sour cream, apple, horseradish, and salt.

2. The sauce is ready to serve now or store it in a covered container in the refrigerator for up to 2 days.

Lemon Vinaigrette

MAKES 2 CUPS

⅓ cup lemon juice

3 tbsp white wine vinegar

3 tbsp minced parsley or chives (optional)

1 tsp honey

1½ tsp salt

½ tsp ground black pepper

1½ cups extra-virgin olive oil

1. Blend the lemon juice, vinegar, parsley or chives (if using), honey, salt, and pepper in a bowl. Add the olive oil gradually while whisking until all of the oil is added and the vinaigrette is smooth.

2. The vinaigrette is ready to use now or it may be stored in a covered container in the refrigerator for up to 3 days.

Making a Disposable Smoker

To intensify the smoky flavor of trout or other ingredients when you don't have a smoker to use, set up a disposable smoker. You'll need two aluminum roasting pans, a rack, and hardwood chips. (See Chapter 1 for more about types of wood for smoking and grilling.)

Dampen the chips or chunks and then make an even layer of them in one of the pans. Set your rack over the chips, and top with the second pan, inverting it to make a domed lid.

Put this assembly over direct heat on the grill until you can smell the smoke. Lift off the lid, place the food you want to smoke on the rack, replace the lid, and continue to smoke for the length of time suggested in your recipe.

GRILLED TUNA

with Salsa Verde

IN THIS simple dish, we prefer the fish rare; simply increase the cooking time if you like your fish more well-done. This dish makes an impressive entrée for guests, yet it's deceptively simple to prepare.

MAKES 6 SERVINGS

2¼ lb yellowfin tuna fillet

3 tbsp olive oil

Ground cumin, to taste

Salt, to taste

Freshly ground black pepper, to taste

½ cup tomatillos, husked and finely chopped

½ jalapeño, seeded and finely chopped

½ cup finely chopped onions

1 garlic clove, finely chopped

½ tbsp honey

Juice of ½ lime

½ bunch cilantro, rinsed, dried, finely chopped

2 teaspoons finely chopped parsley

1. Clean the skin and bloodline from the tuna, if necessary. Slice the tuna into 6 even portions. Brush the tuna steaks with 1 tbsp of the olive oil and season with cumin, salt, and pepper. Refrigerate until needed.

2. Preheat a gas grill to medium. If you are using a charcoal grill, build a fire and let it burn down until the coals are glowing red with a moderate coating of white ash. Spread the coals in an even bed. Clean the cooking grate.

3. To make the salsa verde, heat 2 tbsp olive oil in a large sauté pan over medium heat. Cook the tomatillos, jalapeño, and onion until very brown, about 8 to 10 minutes. Add the garlic and cook briefly. Season to taste with honey, lime, salt, and pepper. Stir in the cilantro and parsley. Reserve until needed.

4. Grill the tuna steaks over direct heat, turning as necessary, until cooked through, about 3 to 4 minutes per side.

5. Serve the tuna at once on a heated platter or individual plates with the salsa verde.

GRILLED RED SNAPPER

with Marinated Jícama and Manchamantel Sauce

THE COMBINATION of smoky grilled fish, tart jícama, and a spicy-sweet fruit sauce is unusual and dramatic.

MAKES 6 SERVINGS

1 cup fresh lime juice

¼ cup chopped cilantro

4 tsp salt

3 cups jícama, peeled and julienned

6 red snapper fillets, skin on, 6 oz each

¼ cup olive oil, or as needed

1 tsp ground black pepper

2 cups Manchamantel Sauce (recipe follows)

1. In a medium-sized bowl, combine the lime juice, cilantro, and 2 tsp salt. Add the jícama and toss the pieces to coat evenly. Refrigerate for 1 hour. Drain the excess lime juice from the jícama.

2. Preheat a grill to high heat. If you are using a charcoal grill, build a fire and let it burn down until the coals are glowing red with a light coating of white ash. Spread the coals in an even bed. Clean the cooking grate.

3. Brush the fillets with the olive oil. Season the snapper on both sides with the remaining salt and the pepper.

4. Grill the snapper, skin-side down, for 4 minutes. Turn the fish once and grill for 3 minutes, or until just opaque throughout. Transfer the fillets to warmed plates, skin-side up.

5. Serve the snapper immediately with the Manchamantel Sauce and the jícama.

Manchamantel Sauce

MANCHAMANTEL TRANSLATES to English as "tablecloth stainer." This sauce has a sweet, tart, and spicy flavor. The tomatoes really round out the flavor and add richness to the sauce. This would be great with any grilled meat or vegetable.

MAKES 2 CUPS

1 dried ancho chile

½ dried guajillo chile

½ tsp olive oil

⅓ cup medium-dice yellow onion

1 tsp minced garlic

¼ pineapple, peeled and cored

2 plum tomatoes

½ Granny Smith, or other tart green apple, peeled and cored

½ Bartlett pear, peeled and cored

½ peach, peeled and pitted

1 tsp lime juice

1 tsp granulated sugar

½ tsp salt

¼ tsp ground cinnamon

Pinch ground allspice

Pinch ground cloves

1. Toast the chiles over a gas flame or in a dry cast-iron skillet over medium heat until puffed, about 1 minute on each side.

2. Place the chiles in a medium-sized saucepan, add enough water to cover, and bring to a boil. Reduce the heat to a simmer; cover, and cook for 15 minutes. Remove the chiles from the cooking liquid with a slotted spoon and set aside. Reserve the cooking liquid.

3. Heat the oil in a small sauté pan over medium heat. Add the onion and sauté until golden, about 8 to 10 minutes. Add the garlic and sauté for 1 minute. *(recipe continues on page 80)*

4. Combine the chiles, onion mixture, and all of the remaining ingredients in a large bowl and toss until mixed. Transfer the mixture to a blender and purée in batches to make a smooth sauce.

5. Pour the sauce into a medium-sized saucepan and bring to a simmer over medium heat. Thin the sauce with a little of the reserved cooking liquid from the chiles, if necessary. If the sauce is too thin, simmer over medium heat until it is thick enough to coat the back of a wooden spoon. Serve the sauce warm.

NOTE: The amount of sauce you will get from this recipe may vary, depending on the sizes of the fruits and tomatoes. If you have more than you need for the red snapper recipe, let the remainder cool, cover, and store in the refrigerator for up to 3 days. Serve the leftover sauce with grilled or roasted pork or chicken.

POULTRY

OULTRY OF ALL types is perfect on the grill. This chapter includes traditional barbecued chicken as well as North African–inspired boneless roasts. Tandoori-style chicken inspired by Indian cuisine and a Korean-inspired bulgogi bring Southeast Asia to your grill. A fiery jerk recipe comes from the Caribbean. Pan smoking on the grill helps you get the taste of real barbecue, even from a gas grill. You can substitute whatever kind of poultry you have on hand for almost any of these recipes. Use the table on page 83 to adjust grilling times.

Selective breeding has dramatically changed the shape, texture, and flavor of birds. Modern poultry-raising practices run the gamut from huge operations with nationally recognized brand names to much smaller farms where birds are free to roam outside in a yard or pen. All birds raised for retail sale, domestic and game birds alike, must be inspected for wholesomeness and safety. Farms and processing plants are inspected regularly. Trained federal or state inspectors check the birds for any visible signs of disease after slaughter.

Although inspection is mandatory, quality grading is elective. The poultry found in your grocery store has most likely been graded "USDA A." This indicates that the bird met specific standards in the areas of meatiness, appearance, and freedom from such defects as broken bones or discoloration. Whole birds are labeled with a specific name—broiler, fryer, roaster—determined by the bird's breed, age, sex, and weight. When you buy poultry, take the time to read the label or talk to the butcher. *Fresh* means that the bird was never chilled below 26°F. If you see the word *Natural* on a package, you should also see a statement explaining exactly what this means: perhaps "no added coloring or artificial ingredients" or "minimally processed." Note, however, that hormones are not a concern, as they are prohibited in the raising of poultry.

Many chefs prefer organic or free-range poultry for a variety of reasons, including health, nutrition, and, perhaps most important, flavor. To qualify their birds as free-range or free-roaming, producers must demonstrate to the USDA that birds have access to the outside. Birds bearing the organic symbol or the word *Organic* are raised using organic management techniques from the second day of life and are certified by an entity such as the National Organic Program (NOP), which meets USDA-approved criteria and has a system for ensuring that those standards are met. And while "free range" does not mean that birds are organically raised, all organically raised birds must be allowed access to the outdoors.

Grilling Temperatures and Times for Poultry

Times listed are for fully cooked birds, with an internal temperature of 165°F. Cook duck slightly longer if you prefer it medium-rare.

Chicken, whole	3 to 3½ pounds	1 hour, indirect medium heat
Chicken, halved	1 to 1½ pounds	1 to 1½ hours, indirect medium heat
Chicken leg pieces, bone-in	6 ounces	10 to 12 minutes, direct medium heat
Chicken thighs, boneless skinless	4 ounces	12 to 15 minutes, direct medium heat
Chicken breast pieces, bone-in	9 ounces	12 to 15 minutes, direct medium heat
Chicken breasts, boneless skinless	6 ounces	10 to 12 minutes, direct medium heat
Cornish game hens, whole	1¼ to 1½ pounds	1 hour, indirect medium heat
Cornish game hens, halved	10 to 12 ounces	35 to 40 minutes, indirect medium heat
Turkey, whole	10 pounds	2 to 2½ hours, indirect medium heat
	12 pounds	2½ to 3 hours, indirect medium heat
	15 pounds	3 hours, indirect medium heat
	18 pounds	3½ hours, indirect medium heat
Turkey breast, bone-in	5 pounds	1½ hours, indirect medium heat
Turkey drumstick, bone-in	12 to 14 ounces	45 minutes to 1 hour, indirect medium heat
Duck, whole	5 pounds	1½ to 2 hours, indirect medium heat
Rabbit pieces, bone-in	4 to 5 pounds	15 to 20 minutes, direct medium heat

Checking Birds for Doneness

➤ Be sure your thermometer is accurate. If you aren't sure, stick the stem of your thermometer into a glass of ice water. The temperature should read 32°F.

➤ Clean the thermometer properly after every use to avoid cross contamination.

➤ Insert the tip of the thermometer's stem at least 1 inch into the meat, avoiding any bones to get an accurate reading. Give the thermometer about 1 minute to come up to temperature.

➤ If your meat is too thin to take an accurate reading with an instant-read thermometer, use the touch test (meats will feel firm to the touch) or cut into a piece.

"BEER CAN" CHICKEN

Use a clean cotton mop to daub the chicken with the mopping sauce as it roasts on the grill.

MAKES 8 SERVINGS

2 fryer chickens, about 4 lb each

4 tsp salt

2 tsp ground black pepper

Two 12-ounce cans lager- or pilsner-style beer

10 tbsp lemon juice

¼ cup Barbecue Sauce (page 41)

1. Preheat a gas grill to medium-high; leave one burner off. If you are using a charcoal grill, build a fire and let it burn down until the coals are glowing red with a moderate coating of white ash. Spread the coals in an even bed on one side of the grill. Clean the cooking grate.

2. Blot the chickens dry and season with 2 tsp of the salt and 1 tsp of the pepper.

3. To make the mopping sauce: Pour half the beer from each can into a bowl. Add the lemon juice, Barbecue Sauce, the remaining 2 tsp salt, and the remaining 1 tsp pepper. Leave each beer can half full of beer and set aside.

4. If you are using vertical roasters, add the reserved beer to the reservoirs in the roasters, assemble the roasters, and set the chickens on the roasters. If cooking the chickens on the beer cans, set the cans on the grill over direct heat and carefully lower the chickens onto them. Position the legs so that they balance the chickens. Grill over direct heat, covered, until golden, mopping the chickens every 10 minutes with the mopping sauce, about 30 minutes. *(recipe continues on page 86)*

LEFT TO RIGHT Position the back of the bird on the vertical roaster and gently roll the front of the chicken over the roaster; push the drumsticks forward until they are almost touching to properly balance the bird. Baste the chicken over medium-high heat until it turns golden brown. As the layers of the mopping sauce build up and caramelize, a rich, flavorful, mahogany crust will form on the chicken. Opposite, the "Beer Can" Chicken here is served with the Grilled Sweet Onions (page 144).

5. Move the chickens to indirect heat, cover, and continue to cook until brown, mopping every 10 to 15 minutes, until they are a rich brown and cooked through (165°F), another 30 to 35 minutes.

6. Remove the chickens from the beer cans or roasters, transfer to a platter, and let rest for 15 minutes.

7. Cut into quarters with a kitchen fork and boning knife. Serve on a heated platter or plates.

About Barbecue Sauce

Barbecue sauce is a grilling basic. There are plenty of good barbecue sauces you can buy, but they are easy to make at home in large enough amounts to last for a couple of weeks of grilling. You can find recipes for a variety of barbecue sauces in this book. You can double or triple those recipes to make batches in the size you require. That way, you'll have plenty to both baste on the food and to pass on the side at the table. (Never serve the sauce you used to baste foods, especially hazardous foods likes poultry, meats, or fish.)

When you are ready to grill, measure out the amount you need and heat it right on the grill, if you have room, or on a burner. It should come to a simmer and stay there for 3 minutes. This step gives you a chance to check the barbecue sauce for flavor and consistency.

Add more seasonings to the barbecue sauce now. One obvious adjustment is salt and pepper. Instead of black pepper, you might want to add some finely minced chiles, a few drops (or more) of your favorite hot sauce, a little cayenne, or red pepper flakes. Citrus

About Beer Can Chicken

"Beer Can" Chicken was a popular trend in outdoor cooking. The idea was that you could replicate a spit by making the chicken stand upright. A typical beer can was just the right size and height. Although it might seem primitive, you can still use a beer can if you don't have the roasting tool we show in our photos. If you like the flavor and the incredibly moist bird you get from "beer can" roasting, it's worth the money to get a vertical roaster, if for no other reason than that you can use all those fabulous juices to baste the bird as it cooks.

juices, vinegars, brewed coffee, and mustard are all good options as basic seasoning adjustments.

The sauce should be thick enough to cling, but not so thick that it covers the food in a heavy layer. As barbecue sauces sit in the refrigerator they can become thicker, so if you need to thin the sauce, use either plain water (add it just a spoonful at a time to the simmering sauce), a broth, beer, or other flavorful liquid until the sauce has a good consistency.

Keep the sauce warm and have a brush at the ready. A 2-inch-wide brush with a long handle is the best choice. You can keep the barbecue sauce right on the grill but pulled to the edge, if there is enough room.

Remember that several light coats produce a richer glaze. Not only that, brushing on just enough to cling means you are less likely to scorch the food you are grilling.

Finally, once you are done grilling, discard any of the sauce you used for glazing. If you want to pass sauce on the side, measure out some more and warm it up.

BLACK JACK CHICKEN BREASTS

THIS IS a traditional backyard favorite that's hard to beat and a great way to show off your barbecue sauce repertoire. Black Jack Barbecue Sauce gets its name from the jolt of strong coffee that is added to it.

MAKES 8 SERVINGS

2 cups apple cider

½ cup cider vinegar

1 tbsp minced shallots

1 tbsp minced garlic

2 tsp salt, or to taste

1 tsp ground black pepper, or to taste

8 chicken breasts, bone in and skin on

2 cups Black Jack Barbecue Sauce (recipe follows)

1. To make the marinade: Combine the apple cider, cider vinegar, shallots, garlic, 1 tsp of the salt, and ½ tsp of the pepper in a zip-close bag. Add the chicken pieces and seal the bag, pressing out the air. Let marinate in the refrigerator for at least 2 and up to 12 hours.

2. Preheat a gas grill to medium-high; leave one burner off. If you are using a charcoal grill, build a fire and let it burn down until the coals are glowing red with a moderate coating of white ash. Spread the coals in an even bed on one side of the grill. Clean the cooking grate.

3. Remove the chicken from the marinade, letting any excess drain off. Season with the remaining salt and pepper.

4. Grill the chicken over direct heat until marked on all sides, about 3 minutes per side. Finish cooking the chicken over indirect heat, covered, turning every few minutes and brushing with the barbecue sauce, until the chicken is cooked through (165°F) and the juices run clear, 10 to 15 minutes more.

5. Serve on a heated platter or plates.

Black Jack Barbecue Sauce

MAKES 4 CUPS

2 tbsp vegetable oil

1 yellow onion, diced small

2 tbsp minced garlic

¼ cup chili powder

2 tbsp minced jalapeño, or to taste

1 cup tomato paste

1 cup brewed coffee

1 cup Worcestershire sauce

½ cup apple cider vinegar

½ cup lightly packed brown sugar

½ cup apple cider or apple juice

1. Heat the vegetable oil in a heavy 2-quart saucepan over medium heat. Add the onion and garlic and sauté until translucent, about 3 minutes. Add the chili powder and jalapeño, and sauté for 1 minute. Add the tomato paste and cook, stirring constantly, for 2 minutes.

2. Add all the remaining ingredients and simmer, stirring occasionally, for 10 to 15 minutes. Use immediately, or let cool to room temperature before storing in a clean, covered container in the refrigerator for up to 1 month.

GRILLED CHICKEN BULGOGI-STYLE

BULGOGI, ALSO spelled Bool Kogi, is a traditional Korean dish consisting of grilled meat served in a wrapper. Usually, bulgogi features beef, a popular meat in Korean cooking, but we've adapted it to chicken thighs. The word *bulgogi* translates as "fire meat," so you can expect some heat. The marinade contains sugar, which can burn quickly over the hot fire necessary to grill the bulgogi, so keep an eye on it as it cooks and move the chicken pieces to a cooler spot if the marinade starts to scorch.

MAKES 8 SERVINGS

1 cup minced scallions

3 tbsp minced ginger

1 tbsp minced garlic

⅓ cup light soy sauce

5 tbsp mirin (sweet rice wine)

1 tbsp vegetable oil

4 tsp toasted sesame seeds

2 tbsp granulated sugar

2 tsp Korean red pepper powder

8 boneless, skinless chicken thighs

½ cup Korean red pepper paste

16 leaves Napa cabbage or iceberg lettuce

Scallion Salad (recipe follows)

3 garlic cloves, thinly sliced and blanched (see note)

1. Whisk together the scallions, ginger, garlic, soy sauce, 3 tbsp of the mirin, the oil, 3 tsp of the sesame seeds, 1 tbsp of the sugar, and the red pepper powder to make a marinade.

2. Trim the chicken thighs to remove any pockets of fat and pound them until they are an even ½ inch thick. Cut each thigh in half. Add the pounded chicken thighs to the marinade and turn to coat the chicken evenly. Let marinate in the refrigerator for at least 1 and up to 12 hours.

3. Smash the remaining 1 tsp sesame seeds and whisk together with the red pepper paste, the remaining 2 tbsp mirin, and the remaining 1 tbsp sugar to make a sauce. Refrigerate the sauce in a covered container until ready to serve.

4. Preheat a gas grill to high. If you are using a charcoal grill, build a fire and let it burn down until the coals are glowing red with a moderate coating of white ash. Spread the coals in an even bed. Clean the cooking grate.

5. Remove the chicken from the marinade, letting any excess marinade drain off. Grill the chicken until browned and cooked through, about 4 to 5 minutes per side.

6. Arrange 2 cabbage or lettuce leaves on each plate. Place a chicken thigh on top, spoon some of the Scallion Salad over it, and garnish with slices of the garlic and the reserved sauce.

To blanch the garlic, bring a small pan of water to a boil. Add the sliced garlic and simmer for 30 seconds. Drain the garlic, rinse with cool water, and drain and rinse again. You can blanch the garlic ahead of time and keep it in the refrigerator until you are ready to use it.

Scallion Salad

MAKES 8 SERVINGS

½ tsp granulated sugar

¼ tsp sesame oil

1 tsp mirin (sweet rice wine)

½ tsp toasted sesame seeds, smashed

½ tsp Korean red pepper powder

1 tsp salt

2 cups scallion julienne

1. Combine the sugar, sesame oil, mirin, sesame seeds, red pepper powder, and salt.

2. Add the scallions and toss together just before serving.

PLUM-GLAZED GRILLED CHICKEN

THIS CHICKEN dish features some classic Asian flavors. The variety, quality, and availability of Asian sauces have improved over the years, to the point where you can find a selection of good-quality brands in most supermarkets. It is still worth the trouble to seek out specialty shops if you are a true aficionado of Asian cooking, though.

MAKES 6 SERVINGS

¼ cup Chinese rice wine or dry sherry wine

¼ cup soy sauce

¼ cup plum sauce

¼ cup water, or more as needed

3 tbsp rice wine vinegar

3 tbsp honey

1 tsp salt

½ tsp ground black pepper

2 fryer chickens, 2½ to 3 lb each, cut into eighths and trimmed

1. Preheat a gas grill to medium-high; leave one burner off. If you are using a charcoal grill, build a fire and let it burn down until the coals are glowing red with a moderate coating of white ash. Spread the coals in an even bed on one side of the grill. Clean the cooking grate.

2. To make the plum glaze: Combine the rice wine, soy sauce, plum sauce, water, vinegar, honey, salt, and pepper in a small saucepan. Bring to a boil over medium heat. Thin the glaze with more water, if needed, so the glaze lightly coats the back of a spoon.

3. Grill the chicken over direct heat on the first side until well browned, 6 to 8 minutes. Move the chicken pieces to indirect heat. Cover and continue to grill the chicken, turning every 5 minutes and brushing with the plum glaze, until cooked through (165°F), about 15 minutes more for the breast pieces and 20 minutes more for drumsticks and thighs.

4. Serve immediately on a heated platter or plates.

GRILLED CINNAMON CHICKEN

CINNAMON STICKS are made from the bark of a tree. As the bark dries, it curls into quills. You can snap long quills into long shards, perfect to use as skewers for this Asian-inspired chicken skewer. It's just as good prepared on wooden skewers, though.

MAKES 8 SERVINGS

8 boneless, skinless chicken breasts, cut into 2-inch cubes

64 cinnamon-stick skewers

⅔ cup sherry wine

⅔ cup plum sauce

4 tsp hoisin sauce

4 tsp soy sauce

8 tsp toasted sesame seeds

⅔ cup thin-sliced scallions, green parts only

1. Thread 1 or 2 of the chicken cubes onto the cinnamon-stick skewers.

2. Combine the sherry, plum sauce, hoisin sauce, and soy sauce. Reserve half of the mixture to use as a dipping sauce. Pour the remainder over the skewered chicken pieces and turn to coat evenly. Cover, and let marinate in the refrigerator for at least 1½ and up to 24 hours (depending on the strength of flavor you want).

3. Heat the reserved dipping sauce in a small sauté pan over medium-high to high heat. Bring the sauce to a boil, reduce to a simmer, and cook until thickened slightly, about 2½ minutes. Keep warm.

4. Preheat a gas grill to high. If you are using a charcoal grill, build a fire and let it burn down until the coals are glowing red with a light coating of white ash. Spread the coals in an even bed. Clean the cooking grate.

5. Grill the chicken skewers covered over direct heat, turning as necessary, until the chicken is browned and is cooked through (165°F), about 12 to 15 minutes.

6. Brush the skewers with some of the dipping sauce and garnish with the sesame seeds and scallions. Serve immediately with the reserved dipping sauce.

PAN-SMOKED CHICKEN

with Apricot-Ancho Barbecue Glaze

To LEARN more about setting yourself up for pan-smoking, see *Making a Disposable Smoker* (page 76).

MAKES 8 SERVINGS

8 boneless chicken breasts or suprêmes (see page 94)

2 tsp salt

1 tsp ground black pepper

1¼ cups vegetable oil

½ cup cider vinegar

2 tbsp Worcestershire sauce

1 tbsp brown sugar

2 tsp dry mustard

1 tsp Tabasco sauce

1 tsp garlic powder

1 tsp onion powder

1 tbsp minced garlic

1 cup Apricot-Ancho Barbecue Glaze (page 20), or as needed

1. Season the chicken with the salt and pepper.

2. Combine the oil, vinegar, Worcestershire, sugar, mustard, Tabasco, garlic powder, onion powder, and minced garlic to make a marinade.

3. Pour the marinade over the chicken, turning the chicken pieces to coat evenly. Cover and let marinate in the refrigerator for at least 3 hours or up to overnight.

(recipe continues on page 94)

LEFT TO RIGHT Place the chicken on the smoker setup on the grill; leave enough space around the chicken to make sure that the smoke circulates properly. Do not smoke the chicken too long or the outside of the chicken will dry out. The Pan-Smoked Chicken shown here is served with Hoe Cakes (page 151); start cooking the Hoe Cakes just before the chicken finishes cooking or while the chicken is resting. Opposite, the Pan-Smoked Chicken and the Hoe Cakes are garnished with a drizzle of extra-virgin olive oil and a sprinkle of chopped herbs.

4. Preheat the grill to medium. If you are using a charcoal grill, build a fire and let it burn down until the coals are glowing red with a light coating of white ash. Spread the coals in an even bed. Clean the cooking grate.

5. Place a rack over lightly dampened hardwood chips in an aluminum pan and place the smoker setup on the grill. Allow the chips to start smoking slightly.

6. Place the chicken on the rack and cover tightly. Smoke until the chicken is light golden brown, 3 minutes. Remove the chicken from the smoker and finishing grilling over direct heat until done (165°F), about 8 to 10 minutes more. Brush the chicken with barbecue glaze about halfway through the cooking time and again before removing it from the grill. Serve with additional barbecue sauce, if desired.

Making Suprêmes

A *suprême* is a chicken breast that has been trimmed and boned in a specific way.

To make a suprême, first, cut the first two joints of the wings away; you can save them for preparing chicken broth. Next, cut through the skin and breast meat along one side of the breast bone.

Use one hand to hold the meat away from the bones and keep making short strokes with the blade of a thin knife along the bones. Try to keep the breast meat as intact as possible and leave as little meat on the bones as you can.

Continue cutting the breast meat away from the bones. When you reach the joint where the wings are attached to the breast, use the tip of your knife to cut through the cartilage in the socket of the joint.

Now you have a large boneless piece of breast meat with just one wing bone still attached. This makes an attractive cut that is easy to handle on the grill. You can remove the skin if you like, but if you leave it on, it gives the tender, lean breast meat some extra protection as it grills.

GRILLED HONEY-SPICE CHICKEN ROAST

THERE IS a distinct flavor combination in this dish that will transport you to Morocco. You can ask the butcher at your market to make a boneless, tied roast from a good-sized chicken. When the bird is rolled up, the diameter should be about 4 inches. You can also use this recipe for boneless turkey breasts; increase the grilling time to completely cook this large roast, however.

MAKES 8 SERVINGS

½ cup olive oil

1 tsp ground cinnamon

1 tsp ground cumin

1 tsp ground coriander

1 tsp crushed saffron threads

1 tsp chili powder

1 tsp ground cayenne pepper

2 fryer chickens, 3 lb each, boned, rolled, and tied

2 tsp salt, or as needed

2 tsp minced garlic

1 cup chicken broth

1½ cups small-dice sweet onion

1¼ cups small-dice carrots

5 tsp honey

¾ cup toasted walnuts (or Candied Walnuts, page 179)

8 slices cantaloupe

1. To make a spice cure for the chicken: Mix together the olive oil with the cinnamon, cumin, coriander, saffron, chili powder, and cayenne. Let the cure rest for 1 hour to allow the flavors to combine.

2. Blot the chickens dry with paper towels. Season with some of the salt and the minced garlic. Brush the chickens with ¼ cup of the spice cure. Cover, and let marinate in the refrigerator for at least 2 and up to 12 hours. (Reserve the remaining ¼ cup of the spice cure for the sauce.)

3. Preheat a gas grill to medium; leave one burner off. If you are using a charcoal grill, build a fire and let it burn down until the coals are glowing red with a moderate coating of white ash. Spread the coals in an even bed on one side of the grill. Clean the cooking grate.

4. Bring the broth to a simmer. Add the onion, carrots, the reserved spice cure, and the honey. Simmer until the sauce is flavorful and reduced by half, about 15 minutes. Adjust seasoning to taste with a little of the remaining salt, if desired. Keep the sauce warm (or, if you made the sauce in advance, cool it and store in a covered container in the refrigerator for up to 3 days).

5. Remove the chicken from the spice cure, letting any excess drain off. Grill the chicken over direct heat until marked on all sides, about 3 minutes per side. Finish the chicken over indirect heat, turning every 10 to 12 minutes, until the chicken is cooked through (165°F) and the juices run clear, 30 to 40 minutes more.

6. Remove the chicken from the grill and allow it to rest for 10 minutes before carving into slices. Garnish the sliced chicken with the walnuts and cantaloupe slices, and serve the reserved sauce on the side.

TANDOORI-STYLE CHICKEN

with Yogurt Masala

TANDOOR IS an Indian style of grilling in which a clay oven is used to cook foods at incredibly high heat. Tandoori paste, a combination of spicing and coloring ingredients, is rubbed into the foods to be prepared in the tandoor oven. They emerge with a brilliant orange-red color. Tandoori chicken, like most Indian foods, is usually served with an assortment of fresh and preserved chutneys. Tandoori chicken is traditionally served on a "salat" of grilled onions and tomatoes, with wedges of lime on the side.

MAKES 8 SERVINGS

2 fryer chickens, 2½ to 3 lb each

3 tbsp lemon juice

1 tbsp salt

1⅓ cup whole-milk yogurt

3 tbsp water

2 tbsp grated ginger

2 tbsp minced garlic

5 tsp ground cumin

2 tsp ground cardamom

2 tsp ground coriander

1½ tsp ground cayenne pepper

½ tsp ground turmeric

¼ cup ghee or clarified butter

8 lime wedges

1. Cut each chicken into 4 pieces (2 whole legs and 2 chicken breasts), leaving the bones in. Peel the skin from the chicken pieces. Cut slits ⅛ inch deep in a crosshatch pattern in the breast and thighs using a sharp knife.

2. Mix together the lemon and salt and rub it over the chicken pieces, pressing the mixture firmly into the slits.

3. Mix together the yogurt, water, ginger, garlic, cumin, cardamom, coriander, cayenne, and turmeric. Spread the mixture evenly over the chicken pieces. Cover, and let marinate in the refrigerator at least 12 and up to 24 hours.

4. Preheat a gas grill to high. If you are using a charcoal grill, build a fire and let it burn down until the coals are glowing red with a light coating of white ash. Spread the coals in an even bed. Clean the cooking grate.

5. Grill the chicken pieces over direct heat, covered, turning as necessary and basting with the ghee, until cooked through and the juices run clear, 20 to 25 minutes. (The breast pieces will cook more quickly than the legs, so remove them as soon as they are cooked through.)

6. Serve the chicken with the lime wedges on a heated platter or plates.

About Ghee

Ghee is a butter used extensively in Indian cooking. You can buy jars of ghee is some stores, but it is easy to make yourself and lasts a long time if you keep it in the refrigerator.

To prepare ghee, cut up unsalted butter and place it in a saucepan. Melt the butter over low heat, then increase the heat slightly. As the butter simmers, you will see that some of the butter has become clear, while at the same time, some foam has risen to the top and some solid material has dropped to the bottom. Skim off the foam and continue to cook the ghee.

Keep a close eye on the color of the solids at the bottom of the butter. As the ghee continues to cook, the solids will turn brown. This gives ghee its special, nutty flavor. Don't let the solids turn black, or your ghee will have a disagreeable burnt flavor.

ROSEMARY-SKEWERED CHICKEN & MUSHROOMS

with Naan

MAKING SKEWERS from the stems of herbs gives the dish an additional layer of flavor that isn't released until you bite into the food.

MAKES 6 SERVINGS

½ cup olive oil

3 tbsp lemon juice

1 tbsp chopped Mediterranean oregano

1 tsp minced garlic

1 tsp salt

½ tsp ground black pepper

12 boneless, skinless chicken thighs

1½ lb mushrooms

12 rosemary skewers (see Herb Skewers, below)

12 Naan (page 170)

1. Whisk together the olive oil, lemon juice, oregano, garlic, ½ tsp of the salt, and ¼ tsp of the pepper to make a marinade.

2. Trim any fat from the chicken meat. Cut the thighs in half and place in a zip-close bag. Pour ⅔ of the marinade over the chicken and toss to coat well. Seal the bag, pressing out the air. Let marinate in the refrigerator for at least 1 and up to 12 hours.

3. Place the mushrooms in another zip-close bag and add the remaining marinade. Toss to coat the mushrooms evenly. Seal the bag, pressing out the air. Let marinate in the refrigerator for 1 hour.

4. Preheat a gas grill to medium. If you are using a charcoal grill, build a fire and let it burn down until the coals are glowing red with a moderate coating of white ash. Spread the coals in an even bed. Clean the cooking grate.

5. Thread the chicken and mushrooms on the rosemary skewers, alternating them. Season the kebabs with the remaining salt and pepper.

6. Grill the kebabs over direct heat, covered, turning to cook evenly, until the chicken is browned and cooked through and the mushrooms are tender, about 15 to 20 minutes.

7. Heat the naan bread briefly over direct heat until warmed, if necessary.

8. Serve the kebabs (removed from the skewers, if desired) with the warmed naan.

Herb Skewers

Rosemary sprigs can grow large enough to act like a skewer. If you grow herbs in your garden, you may find that you have tarragon or oregano sprigs that are sturdy enough to try out as skewers too.

Strip all the leaves from an herb sprig, leaving just a few leaves on the top inch or so. The leaves you strip from the stem can be used for other dishes or you can add them to any marinade you might be using. Thread the food onto the skewer, filling the skewer from the bottom to the top.

Sometimes even the sturdiest of herb stems can't push through some foods. In that case, use a metal or wooden skewer to make the hole, and then push the herb through.

Use a spatula instead of tongs to lift and turn herb-skewered kebabs. They can be a little wobbly on the grill.

GRILLED QUAIL

with Oven-Dried Tomato Couscous

QUAIL IS sometimes sold in a form known as "glove-boned." That means that the meat has been cut and peeled away from the bones in much the same way that you might roll a glove off your hand. Once the glove (or quail) is removed, you simply turn it right side out.

MAKES 8 SERVINGS

½ cup extra-virgin olive oil

3 tbsp minced thyme

3 tbsp minced oregano

1 tbsp minced garlic

½ tsp red pepper flakes

1½ tsp salt

½ tsp ground black pepper

8 semiboneless quail

Oven-Dried Tomato Couscous (recipe follows)

1. Mix together the olive oil, thyme, oregano, garlic, red pepper flakes, ½ tsp of the salt, and ¼ tsp of the black pepper. Brush this mixture evenly over the inside and outside of the quail. Marinate in a covered container in the refrigerator for at least 1 and up to 12 hours.

2. Preheat a gas grill to medium-high; leave one burner off. If you are using a charcoal grill, build a fire and let it burn down until the coals are glowing red with a light coating of white ash. Spread the coals in an even bed on one side of the grill. Clean the cooking grate.

3. Remove the quail from the marinade and brush off any excess marinade. Season with the remaining salt and pepper.

The Grilled Quail with Oven-Dried Tomato Couscous is served with the Grilled Cauliflower with Brown Butter Sauce (page 125).

4. Grill the quail over direct heat until marked on both sides, about 3 to 4 minutes per side. Finish grilling over indirect heat until cooked through (165°F) and the meat springs back when pressed, another 3 to 4 minutes per side.

5. Serve the quail on a heated platter or plates with the Oven-Dried Tomato Couscous.

Oven-Dried Tomato Couscous

TO MAKE oven-dried tomatoes for this dish, simply slice plum tomatoes (or whatever tomato you have that is ripe and fully flavored), place on a lightly greased baking sheet, and bake at 300°F until the tomato slices have dried, about 45 minutes to 1 hour. If you prefer, simply substitute sun-dried tomatoes in this recipe; you can usually find bulk sun-dried tomatoes in the produce section of larger markets. Don't use oil-pack tomatoes, however.

MAKES 8 SERVINGS

3 tbsp olive oil

½ cup minced shallots

1 tbsp minced garlic

2 cups Israeli couscous

4 cups boiling chicken broth

1 cup coarsely chopped oven-dried or sun-dried tomatoes

½ cup grated Parmesan cheese

2 tbsp chopped oregano

½ tsp salt, or to taste

¼ tsp ground black pepper, or to taste

(recipe continues on page 100)

1. Heat the olive oil in a large pan over medium heat. Add the shallots and garlic and sauté, stirring frequently, until tender and translucent, about 5 minutes.

2. Add the couscous and continue to cook, stirring frequently, until it has a toasted color and aroma, 3 to 4 minutes.

3. Add the hot chicken broth to the couscous, stir to separate the grains, and bring the broth back to a boil. Reduce to a simmer, cover, and cook until the couscous is tender, about 8 to 10 minutes.

4. Fold the oven-dried tomatoes, Parmesan, and oregano into the couscous with a fork. Season with the salt and pepper. Serve immediately.

GOAT CHEESE–STUFFED TURKEY BURGERS

with Red Pepper–Apricot Relish

THE GOAT cheese filling in the recipe acts like a wonderful sauce, melting and oozing through the burger when you take a bite. Try this shaping and filling technique for other burgers: beef burgers filled with Gorgonzola, lamb burgers flavored with mint and filled with feta. Soft, ripe, runny cheeses are the best. Chilling the burgers before you grill them gives you the best results, so leave yourself time for that step.

MAKES 8 SERVINGS

3 lb ground turkey

½ cup toasted breadcrumbs

2 tbsp lemon juice

2 tsp grated lemon zest

1 tsp chopped thyme

1 tsp salt

½ tsp ground black pepper

4 oz goat cheese

4 tsp vegetable oil

8 English muffins, toasted

2 cups Red Pepper–Apricot Relish (recipe follows)

1. Combine the turkey, breadcrumbs, lemon juice, lemon zest, thyme, salt, and pepper. Blend well with a wooden spoon. Divide the mixture into 16 equal portions and press into 3-inch patties.

2. Top 8 of the patties with 1 tbsp of the goat cheese each. Place a second patty on top and press down the edges to seal the patties together. Place the patties on a baking sheet, cover, and refrigerate for at least 30 minutes and up to 8 hours to firm.

3. Preheat a gas grill to high. If you are using a charcoal grill, build a fire and let it burn down until the coals are glowing red with a light coating of white ash. Spread the coals in an even bed. Clean the cooking grate.

4. Brush the burgers with the oil and place in a hand rack. Grill the burgers over direct heat until browned on the first side, about 7 to 8 minutes. Turn the burgers and grill on the second side until browned and cooked through, another 7 to 8 minutes.

5. Serve the turkey burgers on the English muffins, topped with the relish.

Red Pepper–Apricot Relish

2 roasted red peppers

¼ cup vegetable oil

1 cup dried apricots

1 cup diced red onion

1 tsp minced garlic

½ cup chicken broth

1 tbsp white vinegar

1 tsp Dijon mustard

2 to 3 drops hot sauce

½ tsp salt

¼ tsp ground black pepper

1 tsp chopped parsley

1. Brush the peppers with 1 tbsp of the oil. Roast the peppers in a 350°F oven until the skin is loose and the peppers have no color, about 1 hour.

2. Peel, seed, and dice the peppers into small cubes.

3. Heat the remaining oil in a medium-sized saucepan over medium heat. Add the apricots, onions, and garlic, and sauté until translucent, about 4 to 5 minutes. Add the red peppers and broth and simmer until most of the liquid has evaporated, 5 to 10 minutes.

4. Add the vinegar, mustard, and hot sauce. Cook until most of the liquid has evaporated, about 1 to 2 minutes. Season the mixture with salt and black pepper.

5. Serve the relish at room temperature or chilled. Add the parsley just before serving.

Roasting Peppers

Anytime you have the grill on with a good hot fire, put a few peppers on to roast to enjoy later on.

Pierce the peppers in a few spots and set them over direct high heat. Turn occasionally until the skin is blistered and charred all over. The peppers will collapse as they grill. Transfer the peppers to a bowl and cover them with plastic wrap. Allow the peppers to cool to room temperature.

To peel and seed the peppers, pull away the skin, using a paring knife or a table knife to scrape off any bits that cling. Cut the peppers in half and pull out the seeds and ribs. Scrape the peppers lightly with a spoon or table knife to remove any seeds or bits of skin that are still clinging to the pepper.

CHICKEN BURGERS

with French-Fried Potatoes

MUSHROOMS ADD moisture and flavor to these burgers. Grind your own chicken meat for the freshest flavor. For a great texture, and a safe burger, make sure all of your ingredients are well-chilled before you blend and shape the burgers.

MAKES 8 SERVINGS

6 tbsp olive oil

1 large shallot, minced

1½ cups mushrooms, minced

1 tbsp chopped flat-leaf parsley

2 tsp salt

1 tsp ground black pepper

2 lb ground chicken meat

3 cups breadcrumbs

1 tbsp chopped chives

1 tbsp chopped oregano

1 tbsp chopped basil

1 tbsp chopped rosemary

½ cup mayonnaise

¼ cup Red Pepper Ketchup (page 187)

1 tsp red pepper flakes

8 Kaiser rolls

2 tbsp melted butter

8 slices provolone cheese

8 strips bacon, cut in half, cooked until crisp

8 leaves lettuce

8 slices tomato

8 slices red onion

French-Fried Potatoes (page 104)

1. Heat the oil in a large sauté pan over medium-high heat. When the pan is hot, add the shallots and sauté until translucent, about 2 minutes. Add the mushrooms and cook until browned and all the moisture has evaporated, about 10 minutes. Remove from heat and add the parsley, 1 tsp of the salt, and ½ tsp of the pepper. Allow to cool to room temperature.

2. Gently mix together the mushroom mixture, the chicken, breadcrumbs, herbs, and the remaining salt and pepper until completely blended. Form into 8 patties. Chill in the refrigerator for 30 minutes.

3. Mix together the mayonnaise, Red Pepper Ketchup, and red pepper flakes to make a rouille. Keep covered in the refrigerator until you are ready to serve the burgers.

4. Preheat a gas grill to medium. If you are using a charcoal grill, build a fire and let it burn down until the coals are glowing red with a moderate coating of white ash. Spread the coals in an even bed. Clean the cooking grate.

5. Brush the inside of the Kaiser rolls with the melted butter and grill until golden brown. Keep warm.

6. Grill the chicken burgers until cooked through, about 6 minutes per side. About 2 minutes after you turn the burgers, top them with a slice of cheese and 2 pieces of bacon. Cover the grill so the cheese will melt.

7. Spread the rouille on the toasted buns and top with the burgers. Garnish the chicken burgers with the lettuce, tomato, and red onion, and serve immediately with the French-Fried Potatoes.

French-Fried Potatoes

MAKES 8 SERVINGS

3½ lb russet potatoes

3 cups vegetable oil, or as needed

Salt, to taste

1. Peel and cut the potatoes into sticks about 1/4 inch square and 3 inches long. (The potatoes may be cut thicker, as desired.) Place the potatoes in cold water until ready to cook to prevent discoloration; rinse, drain, and dry thoroughly.

2. Heat the oil to 300°F in a deep fryer or heavy-gauge pot. Add the potatoes in batches, and blanch until just tender but not browned (the time will vary according to the size of the cuts). Transfer the potatoes to paper towels to drain.

3. Heat the oil to 375°F and fry the potatoes again, until golden brown and cooked through. Drain well on paper towels. Season to taste with salt and serve immediately.

SATEH OF CHICKEN

S ATEH, ALSO spelled satay, is a grilled dish that features lemongrass, curry powder, and fish sauce.

MAKES 8 SERVINGS

3 lb boneless, skinless chicken breasts

½ cup peanut oil

1 lemongrass stalk, tender portion minced

1 tbsp minced garlic

1½ tsp red pepper flakes

1 tbsp curry powder

1 tbsp honey

2 tbsp fish sauce

16 bamboo skewers

Spicy Peanut Sauce (recipe follows)

1. Trim the chicken and cut into thin strips.

2. Combine the peanut oil, lemongrass, garlic, red pepper flakes, curry powder, honey, and fish sauce to make a marinade. Place the marinade in a zip-close bag, add the meat, and toss to coat evenly. Let marinate in the refrigerator for at least 2 and up to 12 hours.

3. Soak the bamboo skewers in cool water for 30 minutes.

4. Preheat a gas grill to high. If you are using a charcoal grill, build a fire and let it burn down until the coals are glowing red with a light coating of white ash. Spread the coals in an even bed. Clean the cooking grate.

5. Remove the chicken from the marinade, letting the excess marinade drain off. Thread the chicken on the skewers, 1 strip per skewer.

6. Grill the skewers over direct heat on the first side just until firm enough to turn, about 1 minute. Turn and grill until cooked through, about 2 minutes more.

7. Serve immediately with the Spicy Peanut Sauce.

Spicy Peanut Sauce

MAKES 8 SERVINGS

2 tbsp peanut oil

½ cup minced yellow onion

¼ cup minced lemongrass, tender part only

1 tbsp minced garlic

1 wild lime leaf

½ tsp red pepper flakes

½ tsp curry powder

1¼ cups coconut milk

½ cup chicken broth, or more as needed

¼ cup creamy peanut butter

2 tbsp tamarind paste

1 tbsp fish sauce

1 tbsp dark brown sugar

2 tsp lime juice

½ tsp salt

¼ tsp ground black pepper

1. Heat the oil in a saucepan over medium-high heat. Add the onion, lemongrass, garlic, lime leaf, red pepper flakes, and curry powder. Sauté until the mixture is well blended and aromatic, about 2 to 3 minutes.

2. Add the coconut milk, chicken broth, peanut butter, tamarind paste, fish sauce, and brown sugar. Simmer until all the flavors are well combined, 15 to 20 minutes. Adjust to desired consistency with chicken broth, if necessary. Adjust the seasoning to taste with lime juice, salt, and pepper, if desired. Discard the lime leaf.

3. Serve the sauce in a small bowl. Store any unused sauce in a covered container in the refrigerator for up to 2 days.

JERKED GAME HENS

with Rice and Beans and Grilled Pineapple–Jícama Salsa

YOU CAN substitute chicken breast, pork chops, or rabbit for the game hens in this recipe; adjust the cooking times accordingly.

MAKES 6 SERVINGS

6 game hens

¾ cup Jerk Rub (recipe follows)

½ tsp salt

Rice and Beans (page 108)

2 cups Grilled Pineapple–Jícama Salsa (page 109)

1. Remove the backbone of each game hen by holding it upright, with the backbone facing you. Run a knife down either side to remove the bone, then lay it on its back and press on the breast to flatten the hen.

2. Rub the jerk seasoning on the game hens to coat evenly. (Wear gloves when working with the jerk seasoning.) Transfer to a shallow pan, cover, and let marinate in the refrigerator for at least 8 and up to 12 hours.

3. Preheat a gas grill to medium. If you are using a charcoal grill, build a fire and let it burn down until the coals are glowing red with a moderate coating of white ash. Spread the coals in an even bed. Clean the cooking grate.

4. Brush off any excess rub from the game hens. Season the hens with the salt. Grill the game hens over direct heat until marked, about 4 minutes per side. Move the hens to indirect heat and continue to grill, covered and turning as needed, until cooked through (165°F), about 12 to 15 minutes more.

5. Serve the game hens on a heated platter or individual plates with the rice and beans on the side and the salsa spooned on top of the hens.

Jerk Rub

MAKE SURE you wear gloves when working with the rub; if the oil from those Scotch bonnets comes anywhere near sensitive skin, it burns like fire.

MAKES ¾ CUP

½ medium yellow onion, chopped

3 scallions, chopped

1 Scotch bonnet, chopped

2 tbsp chopped thyme

2 tsp ground allspice

1½ tsp ground cinnamon

½ tsp ground cloves

½ tsp grated nutmeg

¼ cup dark rum

¼ cup soy sauce

¼ cup vegetable oil

Combine all the ingredients in a blender and purée to a smooth, thick paste. Refrigerate until ready to use. Store any unused rub in a covered container in the refrigerator for up to 3 days.

Rice and Beans

IN SOME parts of the Caribbean, pigeon peas are used to replace the kidney beans here for a dish known as rice and peas.

MAKES 6 SERVINGS

2 slices bacon, diced

1 tbsp minced garlic

1 lb dried red kidney beans, soaked overnight and drained

3 cups chicken broth

1 cup coconut milk

1 cup long-grain white rice

6 scallions, chopped

1 tbsp chopped thyme

½ tsp salt

¼ tsp ground black pepper

1. Cook the bacon over medium heat in a sauté pan until the fat is rendered. Add the garlic and cook until fragrant, about 30 seconds.

2. Add the beans and chicken broth, bring to a simmer, and cover. Cook until tender, about 50 minutes. (This can be done in advance. Cool the cooked beans quickly and store them in their cooking liquid in a covered container in the refrigerator for up to 24 hours.)

3. Add the coconut milk and rice to the beans. Simmer, covered, until the rice is tender to the bite, about 20 minutes.

4. Remove from the heat and fold in the scallions and thyme. Season with the salt and pepper. Serve hot.

Wild and Brown Rice Pilaf

THIS BASIC pilaf has been given an Asian twist with the addition of scallions and sesame seeds, but it can be modified to accompany almost any dish that you would like.

MAKES 6 SERVINGS

1 tbsp vegetable oil

¼ cup minced yellow onion

1 tbsp minced ginger

½ cup wild rice

¾ cup brown rice

1 tsp salt

2½ cups chicken or vegetable broth

½ cup thin-sliced scallions

1½ tbsp sesame seeds (black or white)

1 tbsp sesame oil

1. Heat the vegetable oil in a 2-quart saucepot over medium heat. Add the onion and ginger and sauté until the onion is translucent, about 2 minutes.

2. Add the wild and brown rice to the pan, and toast, stirring constantly, until a nutty aroma arises, about 1 minute. Stir in the salt.

3. Add the broth and bring to a simmer. Reduce heat to low, cover, and simmer until the broth has been absorbed by the rice and it is just tender to the bite, about 40 minutes.

4. Fluff the rice with a fork and fold in the scallions, sesame seeds, and sesame oil. Keep warm until ready to serve.

Grilled Pineapple–Jícama Salsa

WHEN YOU have the grill fired up, toss on a few things to have on hand for quick salsas that feature the flavor of the grill, like this one. To learn more about grilling pineapple, see page 210.

MAKES 4½ CUPS

3 tbsp lime juice

2 tbsp olive oil

2 tbsp chopped cilantro

½ tsp salt, or to taste

½ tsp black pepper, or to taste

2 cups diced grilled pineapple

1 cup jícama julienne

¾ cup small-dice red onion

¾ cup small-dice red pepper

2 tsp minced jalapeño, or to taste

1. Whisk together the lime juice, oil, cilantro, salt, and pepper in a salad bowl. Add the pineapple, jícama, onion, and peppers, and toss to combine well. Adjust seasoning to taste with salt and pepper. Refrigerate the salsa until ready to use. Store any unused salsa in a covered container in the refrigerator for up to 2 days.

Meyer Lemon Salsa

THE MEYER lemon, thought to be a cross between a lemon and an orange, appears to have originated in China over 400 years ago. In 1908, Frank Meyer introduced the fruit in the United States. At first, the trees were popular primarily as ornamental plantings. Today, these juicy lemons with the mellow flavor are getting easier to find in food markets.

MAKES 2 CUPS

1 Meyer lemon

1 cup minced shallots

¾ tsp salt

¼ cup chopped flat-leaf parsley

¼ cup extra-virgin olive oil

¼ tsp ground black pepper

2 tsp Meyer lemon juice, optional

1. Cut the whole lemon, unpeeled, into crosswise slices about ⅛ inch thick. Remove the seeds and cut the slices into ⅛-inch dice. Place the diced lemon in a mixing bowl.

2. Add the shallots and salt to the lemons, and stir to combine. Let the mixture sit at room temperature for 30 minutes.

3. Add the parsley, and gradually whisk in the oil until thoroughly combined. Season with salt and pepper. Add additional lemon juice if desired.

GRILLED BASIL-LEMON CORNISH GAME HENS

with Meyer Lemon Salsa

CORNISH GAME hens are a great size for the grill. Each bird serves one, and it is small enough to cook through without drying out.

MAKES 8 SERVINGS

1 cup lemon juice

¼ cup olive oil

½ cup grated lemon zest

¼ cup basil

¼ cup chopped mint

2 tbsp minced red jalapeño

8 Cornish game hens, halved (see Halving a Bird, below)

2 tbsp salt

1 tsp ground black pepper

1 cup Meyer Lemon Salsa (page 109)

1. Combine the lemon juice, oil, lemon zest, basil, mint, and jalapeño to make a marinade. Place the game hens in a large, shallow pan. Pour the marinade over the top, and turn the hens to coat evenly. Refrigerate for at least 1 hour and up to 12 hours.

2. Preheat a gas grill to medium-high; leave one burner off. If you are using a charcoal grill, build a fire and let it burn down until the coals are glowing red with a moderate coating of white ash. Spread the coals in an even bed on one side of the grill. Clean the cooking grate.

The Grilled Basil-Lemon Cornish Game Hen here is served with Black Bean Cakes (page 152) and Grilled Summer Squash (page 136).

3. Remove the game hens from the marinade and brush off any excess marinade. Season with the salt and pepper.

4. Grill the game hens over direct heat until marked, about 4 minutes per side. Move the hens to indirect heat and continue to grill, covered and turning as needed, until cooked through (165°F), about 12 to 15 minutes more.

5. Serve the game hens on a heated platter or plates with the salsa on top.

Halving a Bird

Remove the wingtips from the wings. Remove the backbone of the game hen by cutting through the ribs on either side of the backbone. Open the bird out flat, with the bones facing up. In the center of the breast is a bone, the keel bone, that holds both sides of the breast together. Cut through the white membrane on the top of the keel bone. Hold the bird with both thumbs on the keel bone and bend the bird to open the bird out even further. The top of the keel bone will pop out enough to make it easy to grip.

Grip the dark head of the keel bone and pull it out. If it breaks, cut around the part that remains to remove it. Remove the wishbone and cut through the skin to separate the game hen in half.

SPIT-ROASTED DUCK

with Orange-Ginger-Soy Glaze and Wild and Brown Rice Pilaf

SPIT-ROASTING IS one of the earliest cooking techniques. A duck on the spit emerges from the grill with a crackling crisp skin and meat that is less greasy than you might anticipate. Cutting the skin helps to render out the fat for lots of flavor without as much grease.

MAKES 6 SERVINGS

2 ducklings

2 cups orange juice

1 cup soy sauce

¼ cup grated ginger

2 tbsp minced garlic

½ cup chopped cilantro

2 tbsp grated orange zest

Salt, to taste

Ground black pepper, to taste

12 thyme sprigs

12 cilantro sprigs

2 parsley sprigs

2 bay leaves

Wild and Brown Rice Pilaf (page 108)

1. Trim the excess fat from the ducklings and remove the gizzard bag. Pat the ducks dry. Score the skin in a crosshatch pattern, and set it in a shallow pan.

2. Combine the orange juice, soy sauce, ginger, and garlic to make a marinade. Pour the marinade over the duck, cover, and refrigerate for at least 2 and up to 12 hours. Turn the ducklings occasionally to marinate evenly.

3. Preheat a gas grill to medium. If you are using a charcoal grill, build a fire and let it burn down until the coals are glowing red with a moderate coating of white ash. Spread the coals in an even bed.

4. Remove the ducks from the marinade and set aside, reserving the marinade.

5. Bring the reserved marinade to a boil in a small saucepan and boil for 3 minutes to make a glaze. Remove from the heat and allow to cool. Add the chopped cilantro and orange zest. Season to taste with salt and pepper.

6. Stuff the cavities of the ducks with the thyme, cilantro, and parsley sprigs, and the bay leaves. Season with salt and pepper. Thread the ducks on the steel rod of the rotisserie. Place the rod on the rotisserie according to the manufacturer's instructions. Be sure to center the ducks on the rod properly or they will roast unevenly

7. Spit-roast the ducks until browned and nearly cooked through (140°F), about 1 to 1½ hours. Brush the ducklings with the glaze and continue to spit-roast, brushing with additional glaze every 8 to 10 minutes, until the ducklings are cooked through (165°F or to the temperature you prefer) and the skin is crisp and a rich brown, another 30 to 45 minutes.

8. Remove the duck from the grill and let rest for 20 minutes before cutting into pieces. Serve on a heated platter or plates with the Wild and Brown Rice Pilaf.

The Spit-Roasted Duck with Orange-Ginger-Soy Glaze is served with Wild and Brown Rice Pilaf (page 108).

PEPPERCORN RABBIT

with Figs Wrapped in Prosciutto

WE'VE TAKEN our inspiration from a classic German dish called *Hasenpfeffer* to produce the richly aromatic and spicy marinade. The figs and prosciutto balance the dish with some salt and sweetness. If you can't find chervil, substitute parsley, chives, or tarragon.

MAKES 8 SERVINGS

2 rabbits, saddles and legs only

1½ cups Peppercorn Marinade (recipe follows)

12 fresh figs, halved

6 slices prosciutto, cut crosswise into quarters

1 tsp extra-virgin olive oil

1 tbsp salt

1 tsp ground black pepper

1 tbsp aged balsamic vinegar

¼ cup minced chervil

1. Place the rabbits in a large zip-close bag and pour 1 cup of the marinade over them. (Reserve the remaining marinade for basting.) Seal the bag and turn to coat evenly. Let marinate in the refrigerator for at least 2 and up to 12 hours.

2. Preheat a gas grill to medium; leave one burner off. If you are using a charcoal grill, build a fire and let it burn down until the coals are glowing red with a moderate coating of white ash. Spread the coals in an even bed on one side of the grill. Clean the cooking grate.

3. Wrap each fig half in a strip of the prosciutto. Drizzle the extra-virgin olive oil over the figs. Set aside.

4. Remove the rabbits from the marinade and season with the salt and pepper. Grill over indirect heat, covered, turning the rabbits every 10 minutes and brushing with some of the reserved marinade, until the meat is cooked through (165°F) with a good glaze, about 35 to 40 minutes. Remove from the heat and let rest for 5 to 10 minutes.

5. Grill the figs on the outer edges of the grill until warmed through, about 1 to 2 minutes. Remove from the heat and drizzle with the balsamic vinegar.

6. Serve the figs alongside the grilled rabbit and garnish with the chervil.

Peppercorn Marinade

MAKES 1½ CUPS

1 cup olive oil

12 cloves

3 cinnamon sticks

6 star anise pods

2 tsp crushed pink peppercorns

2 tsp cracked black peppercorns

12 allspice berries

½ cup balsamic vinegar

2 tsp salt

1 tsp ground black pepper

1. Heat the olive oil, cloves, cinnamon, anise, peppercorns, and allspice berries over low heat just until the oil has warmed through and the aroma of the spices has been released, about 5 minutes. Remove from the heat immediately and let cool to room temperature. Store in a tightly capped bottle or jar in the refrigerator and use it within 3 weeks.

2. Add the balsamic vinegar, salt, and pepper. Refrigerate until ready to use.

VEGETABLES

VEGETABLES ON THE grill aren't so unusual now, though at one time they were rarely if ever cooked on a grill. With careful preparation, and well-chosen flavorings and sauces, these dishes are vibrant and flavorful enough to stand on their own as appetizers or even main courses.

There's a way to grill almost any vegetable, from a leafy vegetable like radicchio or endive to dense vegetables, like beets. Nearly everyone is familiar with such classic grilled vegetables as zucchini, yellow squash, and eggplant, but we've gone well beyond those classics, drawing inspiration from Russia, France, Greece, the Mediterranean, Italy, and the Shakers of Pennsylvania.

CHOOSING VEGETABLES FOR THE GRILL

Look for firm, unblemished vegetables with bright colors. If the leaves are still attached, they should be full, not limp or wilted. Root ends, if any, should be dry. As vegetables travel from the field to the market, they can lose a lot of moisture, changing them from crisp and firm to shriveled and soft. Farmer's markets and farm stands, grocery stores that feature local produce, or, if you have one, your own garden are the best sources for fresh, vibrant vegetables.

Keep vegetables cool until you are ready to cook them, give them a good rinse, and let them dry. It is especially important to let vegetables dry well if they are going to be marinated before grilling.

Denser vegetables can be blanched before cooking in boiling salted water or by steaming until they are slightly tender. This improves the texture and flavor of grilled vegetables by shortening the time on the grill; that way, they don't scorch and dry out on the outside before they are fully cooked on the inside. Another way to approach denser vegetables is to wrap them in foil and put them on the grill to "steam" in their own juices for a more intense flavor.

SWEET CORN

with Roasted Garlic, Scallion, and Lime-Chili Butters

THE FLAVORED butters we suggest here are simple to adjust to feature the flavors you like best. It doesn't make sense to try to make less than 1 cup of flavored butter, but fortunately, flavored butters keep in the freezer for several weeks.

MAKES 8 SERVINGS

2 tbsp vegetable oil

8 ears corn, shucked

2 tsp salt

1 tsp ground black pepper

½ cup Roasted Garlic Butter, Scallion Butter,
    or Lime-Chili Butter (recipes follow)

1. Preheat a gas grill to medium-high. Leave one burner off. If you are using a charcoal grill, build a fire and let it burn down until the coals are glowing red with a moderate coating of white ash. Push the coals to one side of the grill. Clean the cooking grate.

2. Lightly oil the corn and season with salt and pepper. Grill the corn, covered, over indirect heat, turning as neces-

sary, until the corn kernels are soft and grill marked, about 20 to 25 minutes. Remove the corn from the grill. Serve immediately with your choice of butter.

Roasted Garlic Butter

MAKES 1 CUP

2 heads garlic

2 tsp vegetable oil

½ tsp salt

1 cup softened butter

1. Place each head of garlic on a square of aluminum foil large enough to enclose the entire head. Drizzle with the oil, and season with salt. Wrap the garlic in the foil and seal closed to make pouches.

2. Grill over indirect medium heat (or roast in a 400°F oven) until tender and any juices that escape are deep brown, about 30 to 40 minutes. *(recipe continues on page 119)*

LEFT TO RIGHT Work the butter with a wooden spoon or using the paddle attachment in a mixer until it is soft enough to incorporate the flavoring ingredients; mix the ingredients until they are evenly incorporated into the butter. Roll the butter into a rough log inside the plastic wrap. Use a ruler or metal spatula to tighten the plastic wrap around the butter and even out the diameter of the cylinder.

3. Let the garlic cool. Squeeze the roasted cloves from the papery skins, and mash to a paste. Blend with the softened butter, then shape as described below.

Scallion Butter

MAKES 1 CUP

1 cup softened butter

⅓ cup minced scallions

¼ tsp minced garlic

1½ tsp chopped parsley

1½ tsp soy sauce

1½ tsp lemon juice

Blend all the ingredients together, then shape the finished butter as described below.

Lime-Chili Butter

MAKES 1 CUP

1 cup softened butter

3 tbsp lime juice

1½ tsp dried oregano

1½ tsp chili powder

1½ tsp hot chili powder

1½ tsp sweet Hungarian paprika

¼ tsp ground cumin

¼ tsp Worcestershire sauce

2 to 3 dashes Tabasco sauce

Pinch garlic powder

Pinch onion powder

Blend all the ingredients together, then shape the finished butter as described below.

Flavored Butters

Flavored butters, or compound butters as they are also known, are simple to make. You just blend flavoring ingredients into softened butter. We've suggested some flavoring combinations here, but you can let your imagination run wild. Try adding minced sun-dried tomatoes and pesto to the butter (see page 121 for a pesto recipe), olives, capers, fresh herbs of all descriptions, citrus zest, spices, or horseradish. Choose your flavors with an eye to the food you want to serve the butter with, however. The flavor should complement but not overwhelm the dish.

After you blend the butter, it can be handled in a number of different ways. Simply pack it into a small crock or bowl to use as a spread for sandwiches or to add as a finish to grilled vegetables. Another option is to pipe the butter into rosettes, about 1 tbsp each, onto a lined plate or baking sheet, then refrigerate or freeze the rosettes until they are firm.

One efficient option is to shape the mixed butter into a cylinder. Cut a large sheet of plastic wrap. Mound the butter about 3 inches away from one of the long sides of the wrap. Fold the plastic wrap over the mound and then tighten the wrap around the butter. Use a straight edge, like a ruler or the edge of a sheet pan, to tighten up the cylinder to keep the diameter of the log even. Once rolled, twist the ends to press out any remaining air pockets and seal the wrap around the butter. Chill the butter until it is firm enough to slice.

Store flavored butters in the refrigerator for 3 or 4 days. If you plan to hold on to the butter for longer than that, keep it in the freezer for up to 3 weeks.

GRILLED CORN VELVET SOUP

with Lobster

LUMP CRABMEAT may be substituted for the lobster. If you choose to omit the Red Pepper Ketchup, garnish the soup with scallion greens that have been thinly sliced on the diagonal.

MAKES 8 SERVINGS

2 tbsp vegetable oil

6 ears corn, shucked

2 tsp salt, or to taste

1 tsp ground black pepper, or to taste

4 tsp butter

½ cup thin-sliced scallions

2 cups medium-dice yellow onion

2 jalapeños, stemmed, seeded, and minced

2 tbsp minced ginger

6 cups chicken broth

2 thyme sprigs

1⅓ cup heavy cream or evaporated skim milk

3 tbsp soy sauce

½ lb cooked lobster meat (about two 2-pound lobsters)

¼ cup Red Pepper Ketchup (page 187), optional

1. Preheat a gas grill to medium-high. Leave one burner off. If you are using a charcoal grill, build a fire and let it burn down until the coals are glowing red with a moderate coating of white ash. Push the coals to one side of the grill. Clean the cooking grate.

2. Lightly oil the corn and season with salt and pepper. Grill the corn, covered, over indirect heat, turning as necessary, until the corn kernels are soft and grill marked, about 20 to 25 minutes. Remove the corn from the grill.

3. Allow the corn to cool to room temperature. Cut the kernels from the cobs. Scrape cobs to remove any remaining kernels from the cob, catching the juices in a bowl.

4. Melt the butter in a soup pot over low heat; add the scallions, onions, jalapeños, and ginger, and sauté until softened, about 5 minutes. Add the corn kernels (along with any juices you may have scraped from the cob) and cook gently for 2 minutes.

5. Add the broth and thyme. Bring to a simmer and cook until the soup is very flavorful, about 20 minutes. Allow the soup to cool for 10 minutes.

6. Discard the thyme sprigs and purée the soup in a blender until very smooth. Return the soup to a clean pot and stir in the cream. Bring the soup to a bare simmer and add the soy sauce. If the soup is too thick, adjust the consistency with additional chicken broth. Adjust seasoning to taste with salt and pepper.

7. Garnish each serving of soup with the lobster meat and Red Pepper Ketchup.

GRILLED PLUM TOMATOES

with Basil Pesto

THIS IS an ideal dish for summer, when both tomatoes and basil are in such abundance.

MAKES 8 SERVINGS

16 plum tomatoes, halved

2 tbsp olive oil

2 tsp salt

1 tsp ground black pepper

1 cup Basil Pesto (recipe follows)

1. Preheat a gas grill to medium; leave one burner off. If you are using a charcoal grill, build a fire and let it burn down until the coals are glowing red with a moderate coating of white ash. Spread the coals in an even bed on one side of the grill. Clean the cooking grate.

2. Brush the tomatoes with the olive oil and season with the salt and pepper.

3. Grill the tomatoes over indirect heat until cooked through, about 6 minutes per side (start with the cut side facing down).

4. Spoon a mounded teaspoon of the Basil Pesto over each tomato half and serve immediately.

Basil Pesto

MAKES 1 CUP

2 garlic cloves, peeled

1 cup packed basil leaves

1½ tsp grated lemon zest

4 tsp lemon juice

¼ cup toasted pine nuts

¼ cup grated Parmesan cheese

⅛ tsp salt

Pinch ground black pepper

¼ cup olive oil

1. Combine the garlic, basil, lemon zest, lemon juice, pine nuts, Parmesan, salt, and pepper in a food processor; pulse until finely chopped. Add the olive oil in a thin stream with the food processor running and puree until fully incorporated and a thick paste forms.

2. The pesto is ready to serve now or it may be stored in the refrigerator for up to 3 days.

GRILLED ASPARAGUS AND SWEET PEPPERS

CHOOSE THICK spears of asparagus for the grill. The flavor is richer. We strongly suggest peeling the stems for the best texture.

MAKES 8 SERVINGS

2 lb asparagus, trimmed

4 red peppers, cored and quartered

4 thyme sprigs

1 rosemary sprig

2 garlic cloves, sliced

½ cup olive oil

Juice of 1 lemon

Zest of 1 lemon

1 tsp salt

1 tsp ground black pepper

½ tsp crushed red pepper

1. Combine all the ingredients in a zip-close bag. Let marinate in the refrigerator for at least 2 and up to 8 hours.

2. Preheat a gas grill to medium heat. If you are using a charcoal grill, build a fire and let it burn down until the coals are glowing red with a moderate coating of white ash. Spread the coals in an even bed. Clean the cooking grate.

3. Remove the asparagus and peppers from the marinade and grill over direct heat until browned on both sides, about 5 to 7 minutes on each side.

Trimming and Peeling Asparagus

To trim asparagus, hold a spear with both hands and bend the spear until it snaps. Discard the stem end. If your asparagus is too thick to bend easily, you can simply trim away the woody portion of the stem.

Peel asparagus carefully. If you use too much pressure, you could remove too much of the flesh of the asparagus and the spear could snap again. Instead, lay the asparagus flat on your cutting board and then peel, rolling the asparagus to get to all sides. Peel the lower half of each spear. It's easiest if the surface you work on is about 3 inches higher than your worktable or counter. That way, you won't bang your knuckles.

The time it takes to cook asparagus depends on how thick the spears are. It may be necessary to adjust the cooking time so that the asparagus is ready to eat at the same time the peppers are done.

GRILLED ARTICHOKES

with Hazelnut Romesco Sauce

SELECT THE smallest artichokes you can find for this dish. Whatever the size of your artichoke, the leaves should be firmly attached.

MAKES 8 SERVINGS

2 bay leaves

1 lemon, halved

½ tsp salt

½ tsp pepper

8 artichokes

¾ cup olive oil

3 garlic cloves, sliced

2 cups Hazelnut Romesco Sauce (recipe follows)

1. Add the bay leaves and 1 lemon half to 2 quarts of water in a large stockpot. Season with the salt and pepper, and bring to a simmer.

2. Trim the stems of each artichoke and peel them to expose the tender flesh. Remove the outer petals to expose the soft, light green petals toward the center. Slice off the top 1 inch of each artichoke.

3. Add the artichokes to the simmering water. Cover the pan and simmer over medium-low heat until tender, about 20 minutes. Remove the artichokes from the water and allow to cool.

4. Quarter each artichoke and remove the hairy choke from the center of each. Place the artichoke quarters in a zip-close bag. Add the olive oil, garlic, and the juice of the remaining lemon half. Let marinate in the refrigerator for at least 30 minutes and up to 4 hours.

5. Preheat a gas grill to medium heat. If you are using a charcoal grill, build a fire and let it burn down until the coals are glowing red with a moderate coating of white ash. Spread the coals in an even bed. Clean the cooking grate.

6. Remove the artichokes from the marinade and grill uncovered over direct heat, turning often, until golden, about 10 minutes.

7. Serve the artichoke quarters on serving plates with the Hazelnut Romesco Sauce drizzled over the top. *See photo on page 64.*

Hazelnut Romesco Sauce

MAKES 2 CUPS

2 ancho chiles

2 red peppers, roasted (see Roasting Peppers, page 101)

3 garlic cloves

2 tbsp red wine vinegar

1½ tsp Spanish paprika

¼ tsp cayenne pepper

2 tbsp tomato paste

2 cups ground hazelnuts

½ tsp salt, or to taste

1. Place the ancho chiles in a small saucepan and add enough water to cover. Bring to a boil, remove from the heat, and let steep for 20 minutes. Strain the chiles.

2. Combine the chiles, roasted red peppers, garlic, vinegar, paprika, cayenne, tomato paste, and hazelnuts. Purée to a smooth consistency. Let rest overnight in the refrigerator to develop full flavor. Add the salt before serving.

GRILLED CAULIFLOWER

with Brown Butter Sauce

THIS HAS a very different but delicious flavor that might surprise people. The cauliflower gets crispy on the outside and is still a little creamy on the inside. The brown butter sauce adds a nutty flavor and a rich texture and sheen. Very tasty.

MAKES 8 SERVINGS

2 heads cauliflower

½ cup olive oil

2 tsp salt

1 tsp ground black pepper

½ cup butter

1. Preheat a gas grill to medium. If you are using a charcoal grill, build a fire and let it burn down until the coals are glowing red with a moderate coating of white ash. Spread the coals in an even bed. Clean the cooking grate.

2. Cut each cauliflower into ½-inch-thick slices. Trim the thick part of the stem away but leave enough of the stem intact so that the slices don't fall apart.

3. Bring a large pot of water to a boil. Blanch the cauliflower slices until they are half cooked and you can easily stick a paring knife about halfway into the stem of the cauliflower, about 3 to 4 minutes.

4. Drain the cauliflower and let dry for 5 minutes. Brush the cauliflower with the olive oil and season with the salt and pepper.

5. Grill the cauliflower until there are ample grill marks, about 5 minutes. Turn the cauliflower 90 degrees and grill until there are crosshatch marks on the cauliflower, another 5 minutes. Turn over and grill until the slices are tender in the center and they can be pierced easily with a paring knife, about 10 minutes more.

6. Melt the butter in a small pan over medium heat (about 5 minutes before the cauliflower slices are done cooking). Bring the butter to a light simmer, stirring constantly. Continue to simmer the butter while stirring until it turns a light brown and gives off a nutty aroma, 1 to 2 minutes.

7. Serve the cauliflower immediately with the brown butter sauce drizzled over the top. *See photo on page 98.*

MARINATED PEPPER SALAD

with Pine Nuts and Raisins

FEEL FREE to add other ingredients to this dish, including thin slices of celery, fresh basil or cilantro, or red onions. It makes a great accompaniment to grilled, roasted, or baked meats, fish, or poultry.

MAKES 8 SERVINGS

4 red peppers, cored and quartered

4 yellow peppers, cored and quartered

¼ cup olive oil

2 tsp salt, or to taste

1 tsp ground black pepper, or to taste

½ cup extra-virgin olive oil

1 cup golden raisins

1 cup toasted pine nuts

⅓ cup chopped parsley

1 tbsp minced garlic

1. Preheat a gas grill to medium. If you are using a charcoal grill, build a fire and let it burn down until the coals are glowing red with a moderate coating of white ash. Spread the coals in an even bed. Clean the cooking grate.

2. Brush the peppers with the olive oil and season with the salt and pepper.

3. Grill the peppers until marked on each side and tender throughout but not mushy, about 5 minutes per side.

4. Cut the grilled peppers into ¼-inch-thick slices and drain in a sieve or colander for 2 hours.

5. Combine the peppers with the extra-virgin olive oil, raisins, pine nuts, parsley, and garlic. Adjust seasoning to taste with salt and pepper, if desired.

This simple roasted pepper salad can be served as a side dish at a picnic, or try serving a grilled breast of chicken or pork chop on a bed of it.

MIXED GRILL OF GARDEN VEGETABLES

with Three Mediterranean Sauces

THIS IS a vegetarian's dream. Just the grilled vegetables by themselves are fantastic, but with the sauces, they get even tastier. To keep onions from falling apart on the grill, use toothpicks or skewers to pin the layers together.

MAKES 8 SERVINGS

3 artichokes

½ lemon

2 tbsp lemon juice

4 tsp salt

3 fennel bulbs, trimmed and quartered

18 baby carrots, peeled

18 asparagus stalks, trimmed

3 zucchini, trimmed and halved lengthwise

½ cup olive oil

3 tbsp minced garlic

1 tsp ground black pepper

12 new potatoes, parboiled, halved

2 red onions, quartered

18 mushrooms, trimmed

2 red peppers, cored and quartered

2 yellow peppers, cored and quartered

1 cup Italian-style Sauce (recipe follows)

1 cup Greek-style Sauce (recipe follows)

1 cup North African–style Sauce (recipe follows)

1. Remove the tough outer leaves from the artichokes. Cut the stem away from the artichoke, leaving about 1 inch of the stem still attached. Cut the artichokes in half and remove the choke. Rub the cut side of the artichoke with the lemon half.

2. Bring a large pot of water to a boil. Add 1 tbsp of the lemon juice and 1 tsp of the salt. Add the artichokes and simmer until tender, about 10 minutes. Remove the artichokes and let cool to room temperature.

3. Bring a second large pot of water to a rolling boil. Add 2 tsp salt and then, working in batches, add the fennel, carrots, and asparagus, cooking until partially tender, 3 to 4 minutes. Drain all the cooked vegetables well and let cool slightly. Score the flesh of the zucchini with the tines of a fork.

4. Combine the olive oil, garlic, the remaining 1 tsp salt, and the pepper in a large bowl. Add all the parcooked vegetables, the zucchini, the potatoes, and the onions, and toss to coat. Marinate the vegetables in the refrigerator for at least 30 minutes and up to 4 hours.

5. Preheat a gas grill to high. If you are using a charcoal grill, build a fire and let it burn down until the coals are glowing red with a light coating of white ash. Spread the coals in an even bed. Clean the cooking grate.

6. Grill all of the vegetables on both sides until tender but not mushy. Place the vegetables on the grill in the following order: red peppers, yellow peppers, zucchini, carrots, fennel, onions, mushrooms, potatoes, asparagus, and artichokes. Grill the vegetables, turning as necessary, until they begin to take on color and are cooked through, about 8 to 12 minutes, depending on the vegetable.

7. Arrange the grilled vegetables on a platter and drizzle with the remaining lemon juice. Serve with the 3 sauces at room temperature.

The grilled vegetables can be assembled on one platter and dressed with the sauces, or the sauces can be served on the side

Italian-style Sauce

MAKES 1 CUP

2 cups roughly chopped flat-leaf parsley

¼ cup olive oil

1 tbsp grated Parmesan cheese

1 tbsp lemon juice

¾ tsp minced garlic

¾ tsp salt

¼ tsp ground black pepper

Combine all the ingredients. The sauce is ready to serve now or it can be stored in the refrigerator for up to 2 days.

Greek-style Sauce

MAKES 1 CUP

1 cup feta cheese

¼ cup minced dill

¼ cup lemon juice

1 tsp salt

¾ tsp ground black pepper

Combine all the ingredients. Store any unused sauce in the refrigerator for up to 2 days.

North African-style Sauce

MAKES 1 CUP

½ cup olive oil

¼ cup lemon juice

3 tbsp chopped parsley

2 tbsp chopped cilantro

1½ tsp minced garlic

¾ tsp paprika

¾ tsp ground cumin

¾ tsp salt

¼ tsp ground black pepper

Pinch ground cayenne pepper

Combine all the ingredients. Store any unused sauce in the refrigerator for up to 2 days.

GRILLED SHIITAKE MUSHROOMS

with Soy-Sesame Glaze

RESERVE THE stems from fresh shiitake mushrooms, rinse them well, and simmer them in broth until the broth is flavored. Use the infused-broth for a subtle mushroom flavor in other dishes, such as the Grilled Ratatouille on page 137.

MAKES 8 SERVINGS

2 lb shiitake mushrooms, stems removed

8 scallions, left whole

1¼ cups Soy Sesame Glaze (recipe follows)

2 tbsp toasted sesame seeds

1. Wipe the mushroom caps with a soft cloth to clean. If desired, slice large caps in half.

2. Add the mushrooms and scallions to the glaze and marinate in the refrigerator for at least 15 minutes or up to 1 hour.

3. Preheat a gas grill to medium-high. If you are using a charcoal grill, build a fire and let it burn down until the coals are glowing red with a moderate coating of white ash. Spread the coals in an even bed. Clean the cooking grate.

4. Remove the mushrooms and scallions from the glaze, letting any excess glaze drain off. Grill the mushrooms and scallions until marked on all sides and cooked through, about 2 minutes on each side.

5. Sprinkle with the sesame seeds and serve at once.

NOTE: Once grilled, the mushrooms can be returned to the marinade, allowed to cool to room temperature, and added to salads or other dishes as a garnish.

Soy-Sesame Glaze

MAKES 1¼ CUPS

½ cup soy sauce or tamari

¼ cup water

¼ cup peanut or corn oil

¼ cup tahini paste

1 tbsp sesame oil

1 tbsp minced garlic

2 tsp minced ginger

½ tsp crushed red pepper flakes, optional

Combine all the ingredients. Keep the mixture refrigerated until ready to use.

ROASTED ACORN SQUASH

with Grilled Vegetable Ragoût

MAKES 8 SERVINGS

2 acorn squash, halved and seeded

Salt, as needed

Ground black pepper, as needed

1 tbsp softened butter

2 carrots, peeled, cut into thick sticks, and blanched

1 Idaho potato, thickly sliced and parboiled

2 red onions, thickly sliced

6 cremini mushrooms, stems removed

6 asparagus stalks, peeled and blanched

¼ cup vegetable oil

¼ cup heavy cream

1 tbsp chopped dill

1 tbsp roughly chopped parsley

1 tsp chopped basil

1 tbsp sliced chives

¼ cup butter

1. Preheat the oven to 350°F.

2. Season the acorn cavities with salt and pepper. Brush the bottom of a jellyroll pan or baking pan with the softened butter. Place the squash cut-side down in a baking pan and cover the pan with foil. Roast the squash in the oven until the flesh is easily pierced with a fork or the tip of a paring knife, about 1 hour and 10 minutes.

3. Preheat a gas grill to medium. If you are using a charcoal grill, build a fire and let it burn down until the coals are glowing red with a light coating of white ash. Spread the coals in an even bed. Clean the cooking grate.

4. Brush all of the vegetables with the oil and season with salt and pepper. Grill the carrots, potato, onions, mushrooms, and asparagus uncovered over direct heat, turning as necessary, until tender, about 6 to 10 minutes.

5. Remove the vegetables from the grill and let sit until cool enough to handle. Cut the carrot, potato, and onions into ⅓-inch dice. Cut the mushrooms into equal-sized wedges. Cut the asparagus into ⅓-inch-thick slices. Combine all of the vegetables in a large bowl.

6. Bring the cream to a boil in a small saucepan. Add the herbs to the cream, reduce the heat, and simmer until reduced by half, about 10 minutes. Add the butter and stir to melt. Season to taste with salt and pepper. Add this mixture to the roasted vegetables and set aside.

7. Turn the roasted squash cut-side up in the pan. Spoon about 1½ cups of the grilled vegetable ragoût into each cavity. Place the pan in the oven and cook until the filling is heated through, about 10 to 15 minutes. Cut each squash half into quarters and serve immediately.

GRILLED BELGIAN ENDIVE

THE SWEET and sour flavors from the vinegar, soy sauce, and chili sauce are a brilliant counterpoint to Belgian endive's pleasantly bitter taste.

MAKES 8 SERVINGS

½ cup soy sauce

3 tbsp balsamic vinegar

2 tbsp sweet-and-sour chili sauce

½ cup sake or water

½ cup olive oil

2 tbsp fine-grated ginger

¾ cup thin-sliced scallions

3 tbsp minced garlic

8 heads Belgian endive, cleaned and quartered

1. In a large bowl, mix together the soy sauce, balsamic vinegar, chili sauce, sake or water, olive oil, ginger, scallions, and garlic to make a marinade.

2. Place the endive in the marinade and toss to coat. Let marinate in the refrigerator for at least 30 minutes and up to 1 hour.

3. Preheat a gas grill to high. If you are using a charcoal grill, build a fire and let it burn down until the coals are glowing red with a light coating of white ash. Spread the coals in an even bed. Clean the cooking grate.

4. Grill the endive on a perforated grilling pan over the hottest part of the grill with the lid of the grill closed, rotating the pan frequently so that the endive leaves get only slightly charred, about 10 minutes. *See photo on page 61.*

GRILLED RADICCHIO SALAD

with Shaved Jícama, Oranges, and Hazelnut Vinaigrette

RADICCHIO IS a red-leafed Italian chicory with a slightly bitter flavor. Choose heads that have crisp, full-colored leaves with no signs of browning.

MAKES 8 SERVINGS

¼ cup orange juice

2 heads radicchio, quartered

6 tbsp extra-virgin olive oil

1½ tsp salt, or to taste

½ tsp ground black pepper, or to taste

2 jícama, peeled and coarse-grated

3 tbsp minced chives

3 oranges, peeled and cut into segments

½ cup Hazelnut Vinaigrette (recipe follows)

½ tsp red pepper flakes

18 mixed olives, pitted and cut into thin slivers

1. Preheat a gas grill to high. If you are using a charcoal grill, build a fire and let it burn down until the coals are glowing red with a light coating of white ash. Spread the coals in an even bed. Clean the cooking grate.

2. Simmer the orange juice in a small, heavy saucepan over medium heat to reduce by half. Set aside.

3. Coat the radicchio quarters evenly with the olive oil and sprinkle with salt and pepper. Grill over a medium fire until they are wilted and the color has changed, about 6 minutes. Remove the radicchio from the grill and let sit until cool enough to handle. Cut the radicchio into ⅛-inch strips.

If the outside leaves of the radicchio get charred while it is grilling, discard just those outer leaves. They will add an unpleasant bitter flavor to the salad.

4. Mix together the radicchio, jícama, chives, and orange segments. Add the vinaigrette and toss to coat evenly.

5. Mound the salad on a chilled platter or plates and garnish with the pepper flakes and mixed olives. Drizzle with the reduced orange juice and serve immediately.

Hazelnut Vinaigrette

MAKES 2 CUPS

½ cup Champagne vinegar

2 tbsp Dijon mustard

1½ tsp granulated sugar

2 shallots, minced

1¼ cups olive oil

¼ cup hazelnut oil

2 tbsp chopped flat-leaf parsley

1 tbsp minced chives

2 tbsp fine-chopped toasted hazelnuts

1 tsp salt

½ tsp coarse-ground black pepper

1. Combine the vinegar, mustard, sugar, and shallots. Whisk in the oils gradually. Add the herbs and nuts, and season with the salt and pepper.

2. Refrigerate until ready to use. The vinaigrette is ready to serve now or it may be stored in the refrigerator up to 4 days.

GRILLED SUMMER SQUASH

THE SQUASH can be cut into a variety of shapes, from noodles to half-moons to diamonds or triangles, so feel free to experiment. The amount of usable squash may vary, depending on the shape that you choose.

MAKES 8 SERVINGS

4 garlic cloves, minced

½ cup rough-chopped parsley

2 tbsp thyme leaves

½ cup lemon juice

1 cup olive oil

3 tsp salt

1½ tsp ground black pepper

4 zucchini

4 yellow squash

1. Mix together the garlic, parsley, thyme, lemon juice, olive oil, 2 tsp of the salt, and 1 tsp of the pepper to make a marinade.

2. Cut the zucchini and squash lengthwise into ¼-inch-thick strips using a mandoline or a chef's knife. Place the strips in a zip-close bag and pour the marinade over the vegetables. Let marinate in the refrigerator for at least 30 minutes and up to 4 hours.

3. Preheat a gas grill to medium-high. If you are using a charcoal grill, build a fire and let it burn down until the coals are glowing red with a light coating of white ash. Spread the coals in an even bed. Clean the cooking grate.

4. Remove the vegetables from the marinade and allow excess marinade to drain off. Season the slices with the remaining salt and pepper. Grill uncovered over direct heat, turning as necessary, until marked on both sides and tender, about 8 to 10 minutes.

5. Remove the vegetables from the grill and cut lengthwise into ¼-inch-wide julienne to make grilled squash noodles. Serve immediately. *See photo on page 110.*

GRILLED RATATOUILLE

YOU CAN grill all the vegetables for this dish a day or two before you make the ratatouille.

MAKES 8 SERVINGS

1 green pepper, cored and quartered

1 eggplant, trimmed and cut into ½-inch-thick slices

2 zucchini, trimmed and quartered lengthwise

2 cups white mushrooms, stems removed

4 plum tomatoes, halved

½ cup olive oil

Salt, to taste

Ground black pepper, to taste

1 red onion, diced small

1 tbsp minced garlic

1 tbsp tomato paste

½ cup chicken broth

1 tbsp chopped oregano

1 tbsp thyme leaves

2 tsp chopped rosemary

1. Preheat a gas grill to medium heat. If you are using a charcoal grill, build a fire and let it burn down until the coals are glowing red with a light coating of white ash. Spread the coals in an even bed. Clean the cooking grate.

2. Lightly brush the pepper, eggplant, zucchini, mushrooms, and tomatoes with about ¼ cup of the oil and season with salt and pepper.

3. Grill the vegetables until they have grill marks and are tender-crisp, about 5 to 10 minutes, depending on the vegetable. Remove from the grill and let set until cool enough to handle. Roughly chop the vegetables.

4. Heat the remaining oil in a large pan over medium heat. Add the onions and sauté until translucent and just beginning to color, about 5 minutes. Add the garlic and sauté until fragrant, about 1 minute. Add the tomato paste and cook until it turns a deep color and gives off a sweet aroma, 1 to 2 minutes.

5. Add the green pepper, zucchini, mushrooms, eggplant, and tomatoes in that order, allowing each to soften before adding the next.

6. Add the broth, cover, and let the vegetables stew until completely tender, about 15 minutes. Adjust seasoning to taste with salt and pepper, and add the fresh herbs. Serve immediately or cool and store for later use.

GRILLED FENNEL SALAD

with Oranges, Olives, and Cilantro

WHEN YOU can find small fennel bulbs, use them instead. They are more tender and will cook more quickly. You'll need 8 small bulbs to replace the 3 average-sized fennel we used below.

MAKES 8 SERVINGS

3 fennel bulbs

¼ cup thin-sliced red onion

2 tbsp red wine vinegar

⅓ cup orange juice

2 tbsp olive oil

½ tsp salt

¼ tsp ground black pepper

¼ tsp ground coriander

¼ tsp ground cayenne pepper

3 orange slices or segments

⅓ cup oil-cured black olives

1. Preheat a gas grill to medium heat; leave one burner off. If you are using a charcoal grill, build a fire and let it burn down until the coals are glowing red with a light coating of white ash. Spread the coals in an even bed on one side of the grill. Clean the cooking grate.

2. Trim the fennel to remove the tops (reserve some of the fronds for garnish) and some of the root end. Cut the fennel into quarters or sixths, depending upon size. Trim some of the core from each piece, leaving enough of the core to hold the fennel together as it cooks.

3. Combine the red onion with 1 tbsp of the vinegar and let the onions rest until they turn a bright pink, about 20 minutes.

4. Blend together the remaining vinegar, the orange juice, olive oil, salt, pepper, coriander, and cayenne. Add the trimmed fennel and toss to coat evenly. Let marinate in the refrigerator for at least 30 minutes and up to 4 hours.

5. Remove the fennel from the marinade, reserving the marinade to baste the fennel as it grills. Grill the fennel over indirect heat, turning every 10 minutes and brushing with some of marinade, until tender, about 20 minutes.

6. Move the fennel to the hottest part of the grill, and cook over direct heat until the fennel is browned and fully cooked, another 10 to 15 minutes.

7. Combine the grilled fennel with the oranges, olives, and reserved fennel fronds. Drizzle with any remaining marinade, top with the red onions, and serve at room temperature or chilled.

Fennel pairs well with a variety of flavor profiles, so feel free to experiment with ingredients that are available to you.

GRILLED RED PEPPERS

with Orzo Salad Stuffing

WHEN YOU are choosing your peppers at the market, look for ones with slightly tapered bottoms so the peppers will rest at an incline while they are being grilled. Peppers with a blocky, square shape are also good, if you can find them.

MAKES 8 SERVINGS

1⅓ cups small-dice pancetta

4 tbsp olive oil

2 cups diced leeks

Salt, as needed

Ground black pepper, as needed

1¾ cup orzo

1½ cups grated Asiago cheese

2 tsp minced thyme

2 tsp lemon juice, or to taste

8 red peppers

1. Fry the pancetta over medium-low heat in a sauté pan until the fat is rendered and the pancetta is crispy, about 12 minutes. Drain the pancetta on paper towels.

2. Heat 2 tbsp of the olive oil in a medium sauté pan over medium heat and add the leeks to the pan. Cook until slightly browned, about 6 minutes. Lightly season the leeks with salt and pepper.

3. Bring 3 cups water to a boil and season with 1 tsp salt. Add the orzo and cook until just tender to the bite (al dente), about 9 minutes. Drain the pasta and rinse briefly with cold water. Drain well.

4. Transfer the orzo to a bowl and drizzle with 1 tbsp of the olive oil. Add the Asiago, thyme, and lemon juice, and fold the mixture together until evenly blended. Adjust seasoning to taste with additional lemon juice, salt, and pepper, if desired. Set aside.

5. Preheat a gas grill to medium-high; leave one burner off. If you are using a charcoal grill, build a fire and let it burn down until the coals are glowing red with a moderate coating of white ash. Spread the coals in an even bed on one side of the grill.

6. Cut just around the stem of each red pepper with a paring knife and remove the stem and the seeds. Remove the ribs from the peppers as well, if possible. Gently spoon the orzo stuffing into each pepper (about ¾ cup per pepper). The filling should come up to about ¼ inch from the top of each pepper. Brush each pepper with the remaining olive oil and season with salt and pepper.

7. Grill the peppers over indirect heat, turning every 5 minutes, until tender, about 20 minutes. Move the peppers to the hottest part of the grill and cook over direct heat, turning every 2 to 3 minutes, until the filling is heated through and the flesh is tender and slightly charred on the outside, about 10 minutes more. Serve immediately.

GRILLED BEET SALAD

with Walnuts, Cilantro, and Tomatoes

THE WALNUT sauce for this salad draws its inspiration from a Russian favorite, most often paired with grilled or roasted chicken. The heat from the jalapeño can be augmented with a few shakes of red pepper flakes, if you like.

MAKES 8 SERVINGS

12 gold baby beets

12 red baby beets

6 tbsp olive oil, or as needed

Salt, as needed

Ground black pepper, as needed

½ cup thin-sliced red onion

¼ cup red wine vinegar

¼ cup orange juice

1 cup small-dice tomatoes

⅔ cup toasted walnuts

½ cup coarse-chopped cilantro leaves

1 jalapeño, minced

1. Preheat a gas grill to low. If you are using a charcoal grill, build a fire and let it burn down until the coals are glowing red with a heavy coating of white ash. Spread the coals in an even bed on one side of the grill. Clean the cooking grate.

2. Trim the beet greens, leaving 1 inch of the top, and remove the root end. Scrub well under cold running water and pierce each beet once or twice. Lightly coat the beets with about 2 tbsp of the olive oil and season with salt and pepper.

3. Place the beets on the grill over indirect low heat and roast slowly, turning every 15 to 20 minutes, until they look puckered and dark, about 1 hour and 20 minutes.

4. Combine the onions with 1 tbsp of the vinegar and let marinate in the refrigerator until the onions turn a bright pink, about 20 minutes.

5. Let the beets rest until cool enough to handle, then remove the skins. Cut the beets into very thin slices or dice small. (Wear gloves when you are working with beets to keep the juice from staining your hands.)

6. Combine the remaining 4 tbsp olive oil, the remaining 3 tbsp red wine vinegar, the orange juice, ½ tsp salt, and ¼ tsp pepper. Stir in the tomatoes, walnuts, cilantro, jalapeño, and marinated onions. Pour this mixture over the sliced beets and toss gently. Let the beets marinate in the refrigerator for at least 1½ and up to 8 hours before serving.

If you can find candy-stripe beets, substitute them for some of the beets called for in the recipe. They will add another level of color to this already colorful salad.

GRILLED LEEKS

LEEKS TEND to trap dirt and sand in their layers. Be sure to rinse them well in plenty of cool water until all traces are removed.

MAKES 8 SERVINGS

8 leeks

¼ cup olive oil

2 tbsp lemon juice

1 tbsp chopped marjoram

1 tbsp chopped oregano

1 tsp salt

¼ tsp ground black pepper

1. Preheat a gas grill to medium-high; leave one burner off. If you are using a charcoal grill, build a fire and let it burn down until the coals are glowing red with a moderate coating of white ash. Spread the coals in an even bed on one side of the grill. Clean the cooking grate.

2. Trim the leeks to remove the roots and coarse green leaves and rinse thoroughly. (If you are using medium-sized leeks, cut them in half but leave the root end intact.) Let the leeks drain or blot them dry.

3. Combine the olive oil, lemon juice, marjoram, oregano, salt, and pepper to make a marinade.

4. Place the leeks on the grill over indirect heat and brush lightly with some of the marinade. Grill, turning every 5 to 6 minutes and brushing with additional marinade, until the leeks are tender, about 20 to 25 minutes. Move the leeks to the hottest part of the grill and cook until marked on each side, about 2 minutes per side.

5. Serve the leeks immediately on a heated platter, drizzled with any remaining marinade. For a Greek-style variation, top the Grilled Leeks with ¼ cup pitted black olives and ⅓ cup crumbled feta cheese. *See photo on page 43.*

GRILLED SWEET ONIONS

SWEET ONIONS, like Vidalia and Walla-Walla, are perfect for the grill. They have a high moisture and sugar content. This simple dish makes the most of these seasonal treats.

MAKES 8 SERVINGS

4 Vidalia onions

2 tsp salt

1 tsp ground black pepper

½ tsp minced rosemary

½ tsp minced thyme

¼ cup butter

¼ cup balsamic vinegar

1. Preheat a gas grill to medium. If you are using a charcoal grill, build a fire and let it burn down until the coals are glowing red with a moderate coating of white ash. Spread the coals in an even bed on one side of the grill. Clean the cooking grate.

2. Cut eight 12-inch squares of aluminum foil. Peel the onions and trim the root end. (Be careful to leave the core in place in order to hold each onion together as it cooks.) Make 3 or 4 cuts across the top of each onion, cutting only two-thirds of the way down to create 6 to 8 partially cut wedges.

3. Set each onion in the center of a double-layered foil square, root-end down. Sprinkle the onions with the salt, pepper, and herbs, and top each with 1 tbsp butter. Pull the foil up over the onion, creating a pouch and leaving the top of the onion exposed. Pour 1 tbsp vinegar over each onion.

4. Grill the onions over indirect heat until they are very tender, about 1 hour and 30 minutes.

5. Place each onion in an individual bowl. (The onion will spread open like a flower in the bowl.) Pour the juices that have accumulated in the foil pouch over the onion and serve immediately.

SIDES AND SANDWICHES

O F ALL THE techniques that grilling fans have come to know and love over the past few years, those demonstrated in this chapter are among the most exciting, from grilled potatoes to grilled breads to grilled sandwiches and pizzas. The taste of a pizza fresh from the grill and the incomparable texture of a crust that's crisp on the outside and tender on the inside just can't be duplicated in a typical home oven. Other breads can also be prepared on the grill, either by exposing them to direct flame or preparing them on a skillet or griddle that is heated up on the grill.

Cakes and patties made from beans or cooked grains, as well as shaped and grilled polenta, are basics that can be the centerpiece of the menu or round out any menu that features grilled foods.

Some of the dishes in this chapter are grilled right on the grill rack, exposed to the heat from the burner or coals. Others, though, need to be grilled with a bit of protection between the fire and the food. Cast-iron pans and griddles are the perfect accessory for these breads.

To keep your skillets and griddles in good condition, be sure to treat them well. Seasoning them and maintaining them isn't very difficult, but if your pan loses its seasoning or starts to stick, you may need to repeat the steps again.

To season a skillet or griddle for the first time, wash it well with warm soapy water to remove any oily residue. Let it dry thoroughly. Now, place the pan or griddle over a medium-high heat. Add enough oil to liberally coat a skillet; brush the griddle with enough to coat evenly. Continue to heat until the pan is very hot. You may be able to see a bit of smoke.

Carefully take the pan away from the heat and, wearing gloves or oven mitts to protect your hands, rub the skillet or griddle with a wad of paper towel to remove the excess oil.

Once the pan is seasoned, proper maintenance protects the surface you've created. Don't wash a seasoned pan in soapy water. Instead, pour out any fat from the pan and wipe out the residue with paper towel. Add some salt and use a wad of paper towel to scour the pan clean and remove any debris that is sticking to it.

Rinse the pan briefly to remove the salt, wipe the pan dry, and let it dry completely before putting it away.

GRILLED SWEET POTATOES

with Pecan-Molasses Butter

GRILLING BRINGS out the best in sweet potatoes, giving them a touch of crispness and a more intense flavor. The pecan-molasses butter is a great choice, since it echoes the smoky tastes from the grill and harkens back to the traditional savor of a favorite Thanksgiving side dish, without the mini-marshmallows.

MAKES 8 SERVINGS

1 cup softened butter

¼ cup chopped toasted pecans

1 tbsp molasses

2 tsp salt

1½ tsp ground black pepper

4 large sweet potatoes, peeled and thinly sliced

¼ cup vegetable oil, or as needed

1. To make the pecan-molasses butter: Blend together the butter, pecans, and molasses until smooth. Add ¼ tsp of the salt and a pinch of the pepper. Pipe into rosettes or roll into a cylinder (see page 119), and refrigerate until needed.

2. Preheat a gas grill to medium-high; leave one burner off. If you are using a charcoal grill, build a fire and let it burn down until the coals are glowing red with a moderate coating of white ash. Spread the coals in an even bed on one side of the grill. Clean the cooking grate.

3. Brush the sweet potatoes with the oil and season with the remaining salt and pepper.

4. Grill the sweet potatoes over direct heat, turning once, until marked on both sides, about 3 minutes per side. Turn the sweet potatoes over and move to indirect heat. Grill the potatoes, covered and turning as necessary, until tender throughout, about 6 to 8 minutes.

5. Serve the sweet potatoes slices immediately on a heated platter or plates topped with slices or rosettes of the pecan-molasses butter. *See photo on page 33.*

GRILLED HERBED POLENTA

IF YOU prefer, you can cook the polenta in the oven instead of on the stovetop. Once the cornmeal is all moistened, cover the pan and put it in a 350°F oven for about 20 minutes. Give the polenta enough time to firm up and chill before you slice it into pieces for the grill.

MAKES 8 SERVINGS

4 cups chicken broth

1 tsp salt, or to taste

¼ tsp ground black pepper, or to taste

1⅓ cups coarse yellow cornmeal

⅔ cup grated Parmesan cheese

2 tbsp butter

2 tsp chopped rosemary

1¼ tsp chopped thyme

NOTE: *To make soft polenta, decrease the amount of cornmeal to 1 cup. See photo on page 28.*

1. Line the bottom and sides of a half-sheet pan with plastic wrap. You can adjust the dimensions of your pan by adding a temporary wall of aluminum foil placed widthwise.

2. Bring the chicken broth to a boil and season with the salt and pepper. Add the cornmeal in a stream, stirring constantly until it has been all added. Simmer, stirring often, until the polenta starts to pull away slightly from the sides of the pot, about 25 minutes. Remove from the heat and blend in the cheese, butter, rosemary, and thyme. Adjust seasoning with salt and pepper, if desired.

3. Pour the polenta into the prepared pan. Let cool to room temperature, then cover with plastic wrap and refrigerate until cold enough to cut into shapes, at least 1 and up to 24 hours. *(recipe continues on page 150)*

LEFT TO RIGHT Make a wall of aluminum foil to adjust the thickness of the finished polenta, if necessary. Cut the polenta into pieces of any shape that will be big enough to hold up on the grill. Give the polenta a quarter turn while it is grilling on the first side to produce crosshatch marks; this will be the presentation side. The Grilled Herbed Polenta can be paired with a simple green salad for a delicious light lunch, or it can be served with a roast chicken breast for an elegant entrée.

4. Preheat a gas grill to high. If you are using a charcoal grill, build a fire and let it burn down until the coals are glowing red with a light coating of white ash. Spread the coals in an even bed. Clean the cooking grate.

5. Cut the polenta into 12 rectangles, 3 inches by 4 inches. Cut each rectangle in half on the diagonal to make 24 triangles. Grill over direct heat until marked and crisp on the first side, about 4 to 5 minutes. (Rotate the polenta a quarter turn after about each minute of grilling time to give the pieces crosshatch marks, if desired.) Turn the polenta once and finish grilling on the second side, about another 4 to 5 minutes. Serve very hot on a platter.

SKILLET CORNBREAD

with Cheddar Cheese and Grilled Corn

THIS RECIPE may be made with 1 to 1½ cups thawed frozen corn kernels as a substitute for the grilled corn.

MAKES 8 SERVINGS

2 ears corn

¾ cup all-purpose flour

⅓ cup granulated sugar

2 tsp baking powder

1 tsp salt

1 cup cornmeal

2 eggs

1 cup milk or buttermilk

½ cup melted butter

½ cup grated sharp cheddar

1. Preheat a gas grill to medium-high. If you are using a charcoal grill, build a fire and let it burn down until the coals are glowing red with a light coating of white ash. Spread the coals in an even bed. Clean the cooking grate.

2. Trim the stem and loose silk off the ends of the ears of corn, leaving the husks on.

3. Place the corn on the grill, cover, and roast until tender, about 30 to 40 minutes. Give the corn a quarter turn every 10 to 15 minutes. The husks should blacken, but be careful not to burn the kernels.

4. Remove the corn from the grill and let sit until cool enough to handle. Pull off the husks and any remaining silk, and cut the kernels from the cob.

5. Coat the inside of an 8-inch round cast-iron skillet with oil. Place the greased pan on the grill, cover, and let the pan preheat for 10 minutes while mixing the cornbread.

6. Sift together the flour, sugar, baking powder, and salt into a large bowl. Stir in the cornmeal until well blended.

7. Combine the eggs, milk or buttermilk, and melted butter in a small bowl and beat until blended. Pour the wet ingredients into the dry ingredients and mix lightly with a wooden spoon or a rubber spatula just until a moist batter forms. Gently fold in the cheddar and corn kernels.

8. Pour the mixture into the preheated pan on the grill. Cover the grill and cook until the bread is brown and starts to pull away from the sides of the pan, 25 to 30 minutes.

9. Let the cornbread cool slightly, about 5 to 10 minutes, before serving directly from the pan. *See photo on page 25.*

HOE CAKES

HOE CAKES are reputed to have been baked over hot coals on the blade of a hoe—hence the name. A heavy griddle set on top of your grill works even better. For more about using griddles and pans on the grill, see pages 1–4. Try some maple syrup or some of the pecan-molasses butter we've suggested for the Grilled Sweet Potatoes on page 147 as a topping.

MAKES 8 SERVINGS

2 cups fine stone-ground cornmeal

2 tsp baking powder

1 tsp salt

2 cups buttermilk

2 large eggs, lightly beaten

Vegetable oil, as needed

1. Preheat a gas grill to medium-low. If you are using a charcoal grill, build a fire and let it burn down until the coals are glowing red with a generous coating of white ash. Spread the coals in an even bed. Clean the cooking grate.

2. Mix together the cornmeal, baking powder, and salt in a large bowl with a whisk until evenly blended.

3. Blend the buttermilk and eggs in a separate bowl until smooth. Add to the cornmeal mixture all at once and stir just until the dry ingredients are moistened. Use as few strokes as possible.

4. Heat a griddle or cast-iron skillet on the grill until hot. Brush the pan lightly with the oil. Drop about 2 tbsp of the batter for each hoe cake onto the griddle. Continue to drop hoe cakes onto the griddle, leaving about 2 inches between each cake.

5. Cook the cakes on the first side until the bottoms are nicely browned and bubbles form on the tops, about 4 minutes. Turn once and cook until the second side is browned, about 3 to 4 minutes. Transfer the hoe cakes to a platter and keep warm until all the batter has been cooked.

6. Serve at once on a heated platter or plates. *See photo on page 92.*

BLACK BEAN CAKES

YOU CAN cook these cakes on squares of aluminum foil instead of in a skillet, if you prefer.

MAKES 8 SERVINGS

1 lb dried black beans

4 cups chicken broth

1 cup chopped chorizo sausage

⅔ cup medium-dice yellow onion

2 tbsp minced garlic

1 jalapeño, stemmed, seeded, and minced

1 tsp ground cumin

1 tsp chili powder

1 egg, lightly beaten

2 tbsp chopped cilantro

1½ tbsp lime juice

1 tsp salt

½ cup cornmeal

½ cup sour cream

1 cup Chipotle Pico de Gallo (page 72)

1. Soak the beans overnight in enough cold water to cover them by 3 inches.

2. Drain the beans, place in a pot, and add the chicken broth. Bring to a boil, reduce the heat to a simmer, and cook until the beans are tender, about 45 minutes. Drain.

3. Cook the chorizo over medium heat in a sauté pan until the fat is rendered and the chorizo is slightly crispy. Add the onions, garlic, and jalapeño, and sauté until golden, about 8 to 10 minutes.

4. Add the cumin and chili powder, and sauté until fragrant, about 2 minutes. Remove from the heat and allow the mixture to cool.

5. Combine the beans, the chorizo mixture, the egg, cilantro, lime juice, and salt. Mix well, mashing some of the beans (this will help keep the cakes together).

6. Form the mixture into 16 cakes about 2 inches in diameter and ½ inch thick. Dust the cakes lightly with the cornmeal.

7. Preheat the griddle to medium heat on the grill. Cook the cakes until heated through, about 4 to 6 minutes per side. Serve immediately with the sour cream and Chipotle Pico de Gallo. *See photo on page 110.*

GRILLED TOFU

YOU CAN choose any of the barbecue sauces included in this book: Barbecue Sauce (page 41), Vinegar Barbecue Sauce (page 19), Black Jack Barbecue Sauce (page 87), or Apricot-Ancho Barbecue Glaze (page 20) to accompany the tofu. Warm up a little of the sauce and serve it on the side for dipping. Try serving the tofu on a bed of dressed greens and your favorite grilled vegetables from Chapter 5.

MAKES 6 SERVINGS

1 cup granulated sugar

⅓ cup paprika

⅓ cup kosher salt

2 tbsp chili powder

1 tbsp garlic powder

1 tbsp dry mustard

1 tbsp onion powder

¼ tsp ground cayenne pepper

Two 14-oz blocks firm tofu, pressed

¼ cup olive oil, or as needed

1. Preheat a gas grill to medium-high; leave one burner off. If you are using a charcoal grill, build a fire and let it burn down until the coals are glowing red with a moderate coating of white ash. Spread the coals in an even bed on one side of the grill. Clean the cooking grate.

2. Blend together the sugar, paprika, kosher salt, chili powder, garlic powder, dry mustard, onion powder, and cayenne pepper, and place in a shallow pan.

3. Slice each block of tofu in half lengthwise, then cut each half into thirds. You should have 12 pieces. Dredge the tofu pieces in the sugar mixture.

4. Heat a cast-iron skillet or a grill pan over direct heat on the grill and brush with the oil. Add the tofu pieces, leaving enough room between them to flip easily. Cover the grill and cook the tofu over indirect heat, turning the pan and flipping the tofu pieces over as necessary, until the tofu is golden and flavorful with a noticeable crust, 35 to 50 minutes.

5. Serve immediately on a heated platter or plates.

GRILLED POTATO SKEWERS

with Curried Onion Dipping Sauce

CHOOSE POTATOES with relatively similar sizes and shapes for this dish. Or, if you like, use large potatoes, such as Yukon Golds, and cut them into wedges or slices.

MAKES 8 SERVINGS

4 tsp salt, or to taste

24 red bliss potatoes, about 1 inch in diameter

16 wooden skewers

½ cup olive oil

½ tsp ground black pepper, or to taste

1 cup Curried Onion Dipping Sauce (recipe follows)

1. Preheat a gas grill to medium. If you are using a charcoal grill, build a fire and let it burn down until the coals are glowing red with a moderate coating of white ash. Spread the coals in an even bed. Clean the cooking grate.

2. Bring a large pot of water to a rapid boil over high heat in a large pot and add 2 tsp of the salt. Add the potatoes and cook until the potatoes can be pierced with a fork but still offer some resistance, about 10 to 15 minutes (they should

be firm but not crunchy). Drain and let sit until cool enough to handle.

3. Soak the wooden skewers in cool water for 30 minutes.

4. Cut the potatoes in half and thread them on 2 skewers, with the cut sides facing down. Coat the potatoes with the oil and season with the remaining salt and the pepper.

5. Grill over direct heat, turning once, until golden brown with some grill marks, about 5 to 7 minutes. Serve immediately with the Curried Onion Dipping Sauce.

Curried Onion Dipping Sauce

MAKES 2 CUPS

1¾ cups sour cream

3 tbsp curry powder

1 tbsp prepared Dijon mustard

1 tsp salt, or to taste

½ tsp ground black pepper, or to taste

3 tbsp minced scallions or chives

2 tbsp chopped flat-leaf parsley *(recipe continues on page 156)*

LEFT TO RIGHT Thread the potatoes onto 2 skewers so that you can easily flip them over on the grill. Combine all the ingredients for the dipping sauce thoroughly.

1. Stir together all the ingredients. Adjust seasoning to taste with salt and pepper, if desired.

2. Refrigerate until ready to use. Store any unused sauce in a covered container in the refrigerator for up to 3 days.

Potatoes for the Grill

Chefs consider the type of potato they have when they choose a cooking technique. Some potatoes are high in moisture and low in starch—new potatoes or red-skinned potatoes for instance. Purple and fingerling varieties are also typically high in moisture. Even though we tend to think of new potatoes as being quite small, new potatoes are actually any potato with a very thin skin that has been freshly dug. You may find either red- or white-skinned varieties. Sweet potatoes, yams, and some squashes are also relatively high in moisture, which means they can be cooked the same way as high-moisture potatoes. All of these potatoes are great on the grill because they hold their shape well even after they are cooked.

Potatoes that are high in starch, like russet and Idaho potatoes, fall apart easily when they are cooked. To prepare them on the grill, wrap them in foil as described in the recipe for Grilled Potato and Red Onion Fans below.

GRILLED POTATO AND RED ONION FANS

T O MAKE even cuts without cutting all the way through the potato, try placing two chopsticks on either side of the potato; the chopsticks will stop your knife at just the right point, before you cut all the way through the potato. But if you do cut through the potato, don't worry—it will still taste great.

MAKES 8 SERVINGS

8 medium russet potatoes

2 cups sliced red onion

2 tbsp olive oil

2 tsp chopped thyme

1½ tsp salt, or to taste

¾ tsp ground black pepper, or to taste

1. Preheat a gas grill to medium-high. If you are using a charcoal grill, build a fire and let it burn down until the coals are glowing red with a light coating of white ash. Spread the coals out in an even bed on one side of the grill. Clean the cooking grate.

2. Peel the potatoes, and keep them submerged in cold water so they do not discolor. Make parallel slices about ¼ inch apart through the potatoes, without cutting all the way through the potato. Insert some of the red onion into each slice in the potato. This will open up the potato a little.

3. Cut a large sheet of foil and brush the dull side lightly with some of the oil. Arrange the potatoes on the foil (they can be quite close to each other but not touching) and drizzle with the remaining oil, the thyme, salt, and pepper. Close the foil around the potatoes.

4. Grill the potatoes over indirect medium heat, turning every 15 to 20 minutes, until the potatoes are very tender, about 1¼ hours. Serve the potatoes immediately.

GRIDDLED ANGEL BISCUITS

THESE BISCUITS have enough resilience to hold up on a griddle without breaking apart, but they still bake up tender and light because of the yeast. They are perfect candidates for a rolled-in garnish. Or enjoy them with sweet butter and maybe a drizzle of honey or a spoonful of fruit preserves.

MAKES 8 SERVINGS

1 tsp active dry yeast

¼ cup warm water

2½ cups all-purpose flour

2 tbsp granulated sugar

1½ tsp baking powder

½ tsp baking soda

¾ tsp salt

1 cup buttermilk

½ cup melted butter, cooled to room temperature

1. Mix together the yeast and the warm water in a small bowl and let stand for 5 minutes, or until the yeast foams.

2. Combine the flour, sugar, baking powder, baking soda, and salt in a medium-sized bowl, and stir to distribute all of the ingredients evenly. Make a well in the center of the dry ingredients.

3. Add the buttermilk, ⅓ cup of the melted butter, and the hydrated yeast to the well. Quickly stir the ingredients just until a heavy, sticky dough forms. (Do not overmix.)

4. Turn the dough out onto a well-floured surface and pat it into a square, then roll it out to about ½-inch thickness with a rolling pin. Cut into 2-inch circles using a biscuit cutter. Place the biscuits about 1 inch apart on a greased baking sheet. Allow to rise in a warm place covered with plastic wrap or a clean kitchen towel until almost doubled in size, about 45 to 50 minutes.

5. Preheat a gas grill to medium-high. If you are using a charcoal grill, build a fire and let it burn down until the coals are glowing red with a moderate coating of white ash. Spread the coals into an even bed.

6. Heat a cast-iron skillet or a grill pan over direct heat on the grill and brush with some of the remaining butter. Add the biscuits in batches, leaving enough room between them to flip easily. Grill the biscuits, covered, turning the pan and flipping the biscuits over once, about 6 minutes per side. Continue until all of the biscuits are cooked, brushing the pan with more melted butter as needed. Serve immediately.

Rolling Garnishes into Biscuits

When you pat out the biscuit dough the first time, add a garnish such as chopped herbs, grated cheese, or bacon bits by scattering it in an even layer over ⅔ of the dough. Fold the dough in thirds, like a letter.

Turn the dough so that the long side is now parallel to the edge of the work surface and use a rolling pin to make a larger square. Fold the dough in thirds once more and roll out for the final time.

CROSTINI

with Grilled Tomato and Fontina

WHILE THE smoky flavor from the grill is a big part of what makes these crostini so appetizing, you can make them using the broiler instead of a grill to enjoy when the weather isn't on your side.

MAKES 8 SERVINGS

4 plum tomatoes

5 tbsp olive oil

1½ tbsp balsamic vinegar

1¼ tsp chopped marjoram

1¼ tsp salt

½ tsp ground black pepper

½ baguette

1½ cups grated Fontina

2 tbsp marjoram or basil chiffonade

1. Preheat a gas grill to high; leave one burner off. If you are using a charcoal grill, build a fire and let it burn down until the coals are glowing red with a very light coating of white ash. Spread the coals in an even bed on one side of the grill. Clean the cooking grate.

2. Grill the tomatoes over direct heat, turning to char all sides, until the skin blisters and cracks, about 3 minutes. Remove from the grill and let sit until cool enough to handle.

3. Cut the tomatoes into quarters and remove the core and seeds. Transfer to a bowl and fold together with 3 tbsp of the olive oil, the balsamic vinegar, marjoram, salt, and pepper until evenly coated. Let the tomatoes marinate for 10 minutes.

4. Cut the baguette on the diagonal into ¼-inch-thick slices to make 24 slices. Brush each slice with a little of the remaining olive oil, and grill the baguette slices over direct heat until just marked and toasted on one side, about 1 to 2 minutes.

5. Remove the crostini from the grill and top the grilled side with 1 tbsp of the Fontina. Place 1 plum tomato quarter on each crostini. Grill over indirect heat, covered, until the cheese melts, about 3 minutes.

6. Garnish the crostini with the marjoram or basil and serve immediately.

Crostini with Grilled Lamb, Scallions, and Baba Ghanoush (page 160) are shown alongside Crostini with Grilled Tomato and Fontina

CROSTINI

with Grilled Lamb, Scallions, and Baba Ghanoush

THIS COMBINATION of lamb and eggplant draws its inspiration from a Greek classic, moussaka, a layered casserole of lamb and eggplant flavored with garlic and sesame. If the seeds in the eggplant you use for the baba ghanoush are large, you can strain them out. The sauce will have a smoother, lighter consistency if you do. For a peasant-style presentation, just chop the eggplant into a coarse paste, as described below. Grill the eggplant ahead of time when you have the grill already going for something else for a head start on this Middle Eastern–inspired appetizer. If you have some sliced lamb leftover from the Berbere Grilled Leg of Lamb (page 42), use that instead of grilling the lamb chops.

MAKES 8 SERVINGS

3 boneless lamb loin chops

1 tbsp olive oil

½ tsp salt

¼ tsp ground black pepper

½ baguette

¼ cup Roasted Garlic Butter, softened (page 117)

6 scallions, trimmed

¾ cup Baba Ghanoush (recipe follows)

1 tsp lemon juice, or to taste

2 tsp sesame seeds (black and white), or to taste

1. Preheat a gas grill to medium. If you are using a charcoal grill, build a fire and let it burn down until the coals are glowing red with a moderate coating of white ash. Spread the coals in an even bed. Clean the cooking grate.

2. Brush the lamb with the olive oil and season with the salt and pepper. Grill over medium heat until medium-rare inside and brown on the outside, about 5 minutes on each side. Remove the lamb from the grill and let rest.

3. Cut the baguette on the diagonal into ¼-inch-thick slices to make 16 slices. Brush each slice with a little of the Roasted Garlic Butter.

4. Grill the baguette slices until just marked and toasted, about 1 to 2 minutes per side.

5. Grill the scallions, turning occasionally, until marked and tender, about 5 minutes. Cut the scallions into 2-inch pieces (roughly into thirds).

6. Cut the lamb on the bias into ¼-inch-thick pieces. Spread an equal amount of the Baba Ghanoush over each crostini. Place 1 piece of lamb on top of the Baba Ghanoush and cross 2 pieces of scallion over the lamb. Sprinkle a couple of drops of lemon juice on each piece and garnish with sesame seeds. *See photo on page 159.*

Baba Ghanoush

IT'S HARD to make a little bit of baba ghanoush, but you can use it up easily. Besides serving it as a dip with grilled or toasted pita triangles, you can use it as a filling for sandwiches or thin it with a flavorful vegetable broth to make a delicious soup. You can purchase harissa to season the baba ghanoush, but making your own using the recipe below gives it a unique flavor stamp.

MAKES 3 CUPS

1 eggplant

¼ cup minced shallots

4 tsp lemon juice

1 tsp salt

1 tbsp olive oil

2 tbsp tahini paste

2 tbsp chopped flat-leaf parsley

1 tbsp chopped mint

½ tsp minced garlic

¼ tsp ground black pepper

1½ tsp Harissa (recipe follows)

1. Preheat a gas grill to medium. If you are using a charcoal grill, build a fire and let it burn down until the coals are glowing red with a moderate coating of white ash. Spread the coals in an even bed. Clean the cooking grate.

2. Rinse the eggplant and pierce it in 2 or 3 spots. Grill the eggplant over direct heat, turning every 10 to 12 minutes, until the skin is crisp and charred and the eggplant is soft enough to collapse, 30 to 40 minutes. Let cool to room temperature, scoop out the flesh, and chop coarsely.

3. Combine the shallots with the lemon juice and ½ tsp of the salt, and let marinate while the eggplant is grilling.

4. Combine the roasted eggplant and macerated shallots with the olive oil, the tahini, and parsley. Stir in the remaining ½ tsp salt, the mint, garlic, pepper, and Harissa. (Add these ingredients gradually and adjust to suit your taste by adding more, if desired.)

5. Refrigerate until ready to use. Store any unused baba ghanoush in the refrigerator for up to 4 days.

Harissa

THIS SAUCE is a classic condiment throughout North Africa. It has a brick-red color and a potent kick. It keeps well, so have a clean jar with a tight-fitting lid ready to use for a storage container.

MAKES 1 CUP

5 roasted jalapeños, peeled and seeded
   (see Roasting Peppers, page 101)

2 roasted red peppers, peeled and seeded

3 tbsp hot Hungarian paprika

1½ tsp toasted cumin seeds

1 tbsp minced garlic

1 tsp ground cayenne pepper

¾ cup olive oil

3 tbsp lemon juice, or to taste

½ tsp salt, or to taste

1. Combine the jalapeños, peppers, paprika, cumin, garlic, and cayenne in a blender. Blend to a pastelike consistency.

2. Transfer the jalapeño mixture to a bowl and slowly whisk in the oil to create a smooth sauce. Add the lemon juice and salt to taste. Refrigerate until ready to use. Store any unused harissa in a clean storage container in the refrigerator for up to 2 weeks.

GRILLED CHICKEN BURRITOS

with Tomatillo Salsa

TOMATILLOS ARE small tomatolike vegetables that add a tart, citrus flavor to the salsa. Be sure to choose tomatillos that are firm and green beneath the husk.

MAKES 8 SERVINGS

¼ cup lime juice

¼ cup vegetable oil

1 tbsp minced garlic

¼ cup fine-chopped cilantro

1 tsp ground cumin

1 tsp salt

½ tsp ground black pepper

4 boneless, skinless chicken breasts

8 flour tortillas, 10 inches in diameter

2 cups refried beans, heated

2 cups cooked rice

2 cups queso blanco (white Mexican cheese)

2 cups Guacamole (page 35)

2 cups Tomatillo Salsa (recipe follows)

½ cup sour cream

1. Combine the lime juice, oil, garlic, cilantro, cumin, salt, and pepper to make a marinade.

2. Blot the chicken dry and place in a zip-close bag. Pour the marinade over the breasts, seal the bag, and let marinate in the refrigerator for 3 and up to 12 hours.

3. Preheat a gas grill to medium-high. If you are using a charcoal grill, build a fire and let it burn down until the coals are glowing red with a moderate coating of white ash. Spread the coals into an even bed.

4. Grill the chicken, covered, until cooked through, about 5 minutes per side. Remove from the grill and let rest for 5 minutes. Slice on the bias to the desired thickness.

5. Heat the tortillas on the grill for about 30 seconds per side. Spread the refried beans on the tortillas. Add the chicken slices, rice, cheese, and guacamole. Top with the Tomatillo Salsa and sour cream, and serve immediately.

Tomatillo Salsa

MAKES 3 CUPS

1 lb tomatillos, coarsely chopped

1 roasted jalapeño, peeled and seeded
   (see Roasting Peppers, page 101)

1 cup chopped tomato

½ red onion, diced small

¼ cup chopped cilantro

2 tbsp lime juice

1 tbsp minced garlic

2 tsp dried oregano

1 tsp ground cumin

½ tsp salt, or to taste

Combine all of the ingredients in a bowl and toss well. Adjust seasoning with salt to taste. The salsa is ready to serve now or it may be stored in the refrigerator for up to 3 days.

GRILLED CUBANO SANDWICH

THE CUBANO sandwich migrated to Florida with Cuban immigrants over a century ago. Refer to the Pulled Pork Barbecue Sandwich recipe on page 19 for instructions on preparing the pulled pork.

MAKES 8 SERVINGS

8 hero rolls, 10 inches

½ cup melted butter

½ cup mayonnaise

½ cup Dijon mustard

16 slices Swiss cheese

16 slices ham

1½ lb pulled pork

16 leaves Boston lettuce (about 2 heads)

24 slices plum tomatoes (about 3 tomatoes)

16 slices kosher dill pickles (about 3 pickles)

1. Preheat a gas grill to medium-low heat. If you are using a charcoal grill, build a fire with a very small amount of coals and let it burn down until the coals are glowing red with a moderate coating of white ash. Spread the coals out in an even bed.

2. Brush the outsides of the rolls with the butter. Spread the mayonnaise on 1 side of each roll and the mustard on the other. On 1 side of each roll, layer 2 slices of the cheese, 2 slices of ham, and 2 to 3 ounces of the pulled pork. On the opposite side of the roll, layer 2 lettuce leaves, 3 tomatoes slices, and 2 pickle slices.

3. Grill the sandwiches open-faced over direct heat until the bread is golden brown and the cheese has melted, about 45 to 90 seconds. Be sure to grill the sandwich just until it is heated through so that the lettuce stays crisp and doesn't wilt.

4. Close up the sandwiches and serve immediately.

Mayonnaise

For many people, the idea of mayonnaise at an outdoor picnic is cause for concern. Since the sauce is traditionally made with uncooked egg yolks, there is every reason to be vigilant. If you always take steps to keep your foods safe, whether you are putting them away from the grocery store, getting them ready for the grill, or putting them on the table to serve, there is no need to give up this wonderful sauce.

Instead of a mayonnaise made with uncooked yolks, use store-bought mayonnaise, which is made with pasteurized eggs, or use pasteurized yolks, found in the dairy case, to make your own.

To keep purchased mayonnaise safe, always use clean utensils to remove the mayonnaise from the jar. Clean off the rim of the jar and the lid. If your mayonnaise is in the refrigerator for more than 6 weeks, get a new (and smaller) jar to replace it.

Your own homemade mayonnaise won't last quite that long, but as long as you keep it cold, it will last for about 10 days.

Any dish you make that includes mayonnaise, whether it be a spread, a dip, or a dressing, should never be eaten after it has been at room temperature for more than 2 hours. Throw it away.

GRILLED VEGETABLE SANDWICH

with Manchego

A FLAVORED MAYONNAISE adds a great deal to this sandwich. You can blend a number of flavorings into a prepared mayonnaise or homemade mayonnaise (see page 165 for more about mayonnaise). Use toothpicks or skewers to hold the sliced red onion together as you grill it so the slices won't separate into rings.

MAKES 8 SERVINGS

2 chayote squash

3 tsp salt

1 medium eggplant, peeled (if desired) and thinly sliced (about 20 slices)

1½ cups olive oil

¼ cup Dijon mustard

¼ cup chopped oregano

¼ cup chopped thyme

2 tbsp minced garlic

1 tbsp minced serrano chile

½ tsp ground black pepper

4 red onions, thickly sliced

4 red peppers, halved and seeded

4 poblanos, halved and seeded

4 portabella mushroom caps, gills removed

8 hoagie rolls

1 cup mayonnaise

1½ lb thinly sliced manchego cheese

1. Parboil the chayote in boiling water seasoned with 1 tsp of the salt. Cook until tender enough to pierce easily up to ¼ inch, about 15 minutes. Remove from the water and rinse with cool water to prevent them from overcooking and to make them easier to handle. Halve the chayotes and remove the peel and large seed. Cut into ¼-inch-thick slices and set aside.

2. Place the eggplant slices in a colander and set the colander over a bowl or pan. Scatter 1 tsp of the salt over the eggplant and allow to drain for about 20 minutes. Rinse and drain well.

3. Combine the olive oil, mustard, oregano, thyme, garlic, chile, the remaining 1 tsp salt, and the pepper in a large bowl. Add the chayote, eggplant, red onions, red peppers, poblanos, and portabellas; turn to coat. Let marinate in the refrigerator for at least 30 minutes and up to 2 hours.

4. Preheat a gas grill to medium-high; leave one burner off. If you are using a charcoal grill, build a fire and let it burn down until the coals are glowing red with a moderate coating of white ash. Spread the coals in an even bed on one side of the grill. Clean the cooking grate.

5. Grill the vegetables over direct heat until marked, about 2 to 3 minutes on each side. Move the vegetables to indirect heat and continue to grill, covered and turning as necessary, until tender, about 10 to 15 minutes more. (Grilling times will vary for each of the vegetables.) Slice the portabella caps into ¼-inch-thick slices.

6. Cut the hoagie rolls in half lengthwise and spread generously with the mayonnaise. Add the vegetables in layers to fill each sandwich, and top with the cheese. Close up the sandwiches and serve immediately. Optionally, wrap the sandwiches tightly in aluminum foil and return them to the grill to warm over indirect heat for about 10 minutes before serving.

GRILLED PIZZA

SAUTÉ OR grill the onions for the pizza before you begin. You can use uncooked onions, if you prefer. In that case, use a sweet onion like Walla Walla or Vidalia. The tomato sauce that you use for the pizza should not be too watery.

MAKES 8 SERVINGS

2½ tsp active dry yeast

2 cups warm water

3½ cups all-purpose flour

1 cup semolina flour, plus extra for dusting

1 tbsp salt

¼ cup olive oil

1½ cups tomato sauce

2 cups grated mozzarella

¼ cup sautéed diced onions

2 tbsp basil chiffonade

1. Combine the yeast and water in a bowl and stir to dissolve. Let the mixture sit until a thick foam forms.

2. Add the flours and the salt to the yeast and stir by hand, or mix on medium speed in an electric mixer using the dough hook attachment, until the dough is smooth and elastic, about 5 minutes.

3. Transfer the dough to a second bowl that has been lightly oiled. Cover the dough with a clean kitchen towel and let rest at room temperature until nearly doubled in size, about 1½ hours.

4. Gently fold the dough over and allow it to rise for another 45 minutes.

5. Preheat a gas grill to high. If you are using a charcoal grill, build a fire and let it burn down until the coals are glowing red with a moderate coating of white ash. Spread the coals in an even bed. Clean the cooking grate.

6. Roll or stretch the dough into a 12-inch round. Lightly dust a 12-inch pizza pan with semolina flour and lay the dough round on top. Brush some of the olive oil over the entire dough round.

7. Lift the dough from the pan and place the pizza dough directly on the grill with the oiled side face-down. Brush the dough with the remaining olive oil. Grill the pizza until the dough is marked and it puffs up slightly, 3 to 4 minutes. Flip the pizza over and spread the sauce evenly over the round, leaving a ½-inch border around the outside edges. Evenly sprinkle the cheese over the sauce and top with the onions. Close the lid on the grill. Cook the pizza until the crust is golden brown and the cheese is slightly brown and bubbly, about 2 to 3 minutes more.

8. Remove the pizza from the grill and sprinkle the basil chiffonade on top. Cut the pizza into 8 slices and serve immediately.

NAAN

NAAN IS a perfect bread for the grill. The rising and shaping time for the dough is less than 2 hours, and it cooks in less than 10 minutes. You can use any leftovers in a bread salad. Tear or cut the naan into bite-sized pieces and toss together with diced tomatoes, cucumbers, parsley, basil, and a red wine vinaigrette.

MAKES 8 SERVINGS

2½ tsp active dry yeast

¾ cup water

3 cups all-purpose flour

⅓ cup plain yogurt

¼ cup vegetable oil

1 egg, lightly beaten

2 tbsp granulated sugar

1½ tsp salt

¼ cup melted butter

2 tbsp poppy seeds

1. Combine the yeast and water in a bowl and stir to dissolve. Let the mixture sit until a thick foam forms.

2. Add the flour, yogurt, oil, egg, sugar, and salt, and stir by hand, or mix on low speed in an electric mixer using the dough hook attachment, until very smooth and elastic but still soft and slightly sticky.

3. Transfer the dough to a second bowl that has been lightly oiled. Cover the dough with a clean kitchen towel and let rest at room temperature until nearly doubled in size, about 1 hour.

4. Gently press down the dough to release any trapped gas. Divide the dough into 8 pieces. Shape the pieces into rounds and then flatten into disks about 4 inches in diameter. Set them on a lightly floured board and cover with a clean towel. Let the dough rest for 15 to 20 minutes.

5. Preheat a gas grill to medium-high; leave one burner off. If you are using a charcoal grill, build a fire and let it burn down until the coals are glowing red with a moderate coating of white ash. Spread the coals in an even bed on one side of the grill. Clean the cooking grate. Spray 2 baking sheets with cooking spray.

6. Gently stretch each piece of dough into a 7-inch disk. The center should be about ¼ inch thick and the outside edge should be closer to ½ inch thick. Pull 1 edge out to elongate it and make a teardrop shape. Place the naans on the baking sheets, brush the tops with the melted butter, and sprinkle the poppy seeds on top.

7. Transfer the dough from the baking sheet to the grill and cook over direct heat, poppy-seed-side down, until stiffened and golden brown, about 2 minutes. Turn the bread over and grill over indirect heat until baked through, about 8 minutes more. Lower the heat or move the breads to keep them from browning too much before they finish grilling. Repeat until all the naan is cooked. Serve the naan immediately.

BREAKFAST

MAKING BREAKFAST ON the grill is a great way to get out of the kitchen and into the middle of whatever is going on, rather than being stuck in the kitchen all alone. And of course, if you are camping, then outdoors at the grill is the only place to cook! We've gathered together a number of recipes that extend your grilled breakfast options far beyond a pot of campfire coffee and a simple pan of scrambled eggs.

We've used cast-iron griddles and skillets set over a fire to prepare most of these dishes. Cast iron is a perfect choice for camping, since you don't need soap and water to clean it. Scrubbing them off with salt and some paper towel is the best way to remove any surface debris or residue between uses.

To brew "campfire coffee," bring the water to a boil in a metal coffee pot or saucepan, then add the ground coffee. Let the coffee steep off the heat for about 5 minutes. The grounds will settle and you can pour the coffee carefully into mugs.

THICK-SLICED GRIDDLED TOAST

with Apricot and Lemon-Cardamom Butters

T HIS MAKES a great breakfast for the campsite, if you have the cooler space to bring along the already prepared flavored butters. If you don't have a griddle, you can toast the bread directly on a rack over the fire. Or, spear the unbuttered bread on a cleaned hardwood stick and hold it over the flame until golden, then slather with the butters.

MAKES 8 SERVINGS

1 cup softened Lemon-Cardamom Butter (recipe follows)

16 slices sourdough bread, about 1 inch thick

1 cup Apricot Butter (recipe follows)

1. Preheat a gas grill to medium. If you are using a charcoal grill, build a fire and let it burn down until the coals are glowing red with a moderate coating of white ash. Spread the coals in an even bed.

2. Place a griddle on the grill and preheat to medium-high heat. Spread the Lemon-Cardamom Butter on both sides of all the slices of bread.

3. Griddle the bread until golden brown, about 2 minutes on each side. Serve with the Apricot Butter.

Lemon-Cardamom Butter

MAKES 1 CUP

1 cup softened butter

2 tbsp honey, or as needed

1 tbsp lemon juice

½ tsp ground cardamom

¼ tsp grated lemon zest

Mix together the butter, honey, lemon juice, cardamom, and lemon zest until evenly blended. This can be prepared in advance and stored in the refrigerator for up to 3 days. (For more about flavored butters, see page 119.)

Apricot Butter

T HIS BUTTER stores well in the refrigerator, so if apricots are plentiful, double or triple this recipe. Use containers that are perfectly clean and have tight-fitting lids.

MAKES 1½ CUPS

4½ cups sliced fresh apricots

¾ cup apricot nectar

½ cup granulated sugar

½ tsp ground cardamom

¼ tsp ground cinnamon

¼ tsp grated lemon zest

⅛ tsp salt

1. Combine the apricot slices and nectar in a large, heavy-bottomed saucepan; cover and bring the mixture to a simmer over medium heat. Simmer until the apricots are a soft pulp, about 25 minutes.

2. Push the apricots through a food mill or strainer into a clean saucepan. Add the sugar, cardamom, cinnamon, lemon zest, and salt. Simmer over medium-low heat, stirring frequently, until very thick, about 1 hour and 30 minutes.

3. Let cool completely before using. Store any unused butter in the refrigerator for up to 2 weeks.

FRENCH TOAST

with Honey-Orange Butter and Orange Suprêmes

USE AN enriched bread like brioche or challah for the richest tasting French toast.

MAKES 8 SERVINGS

24 slices challah or brioche, about ¼ to ½ inch thick

3 cups milk

7 eggs

3 tbsp sugar

Pinch ground cinnamon, optional

Pinch ground nutmeg, optional

Salt, as needed

Vegetable oil, as needed

Confectioners' sugar, for dusting

32 orange suprêmes (see Making Citrus Suprêmes, below)

½ cup Honey-Orange Butter (recipe follows)

1. Place the bread slices on sheet pans and let dry overnight at room temperature, or in a 200°F oven for 1 hour.

2. Preheat a gas grill to medium. If you are using a charcoal grill, build a fire and let it burn down until the coals are glowing red with a moderate coating of white ash. Spread the coals in an even bed.

3. Combine the milk, eggs, sugar, cinnamon, and nutmeg, if using, and salt to taste; mix into a smooth batter. Refrigerate until needed.

4. Preheat the griddle to medium on the grill. Grease the griddle lightly with some of the vegetable oil.

5. Dip the bread into the batter, coating the slices evenly. Griddle the slices on 1 side until evenly browned, then turn and brown the other side, about 2 minutes per side.

6. Dust the French toast with the confectioners' sugar and garnish with the orange suprêmes. Serve immediately with the Honey-Orange Butter.

Honey Orange Butter

MAKES 1 CUP

1 cup softened butter

¼ tsp orange zest

1½ tsp orange juice

2 tbsp honey

Combine all the ingredients and blend until smooth. Pipe into rosettes or roll into a cylinder (see page 119) and refrigerate until needed. Store any unused butter in the refrigerator for up to 4 days or freeze for up to 4 weeks.

Making Citrus Suprêmes

You can simply peel an orange and then separate it into segments or cut it into slices or dice it, but a citrus suprême is a more refined way to serve the fruit as part of a dish. To make suprêmes, use a sharp paring knife to cut away the peel and all of the underlying pith (the white portion of the peel). You should cut into the flesh, but leave as much of the fruit as possible still intact.

Work over a bowl to catch the juices and the segments as you make the suprêmes. To cut suprêmes, hold the fruit in one hand and with the other, make careful cuts along the membranes that separate the segments, first on one side of the segment and then on the other. This releases the fruit from the membranes into the bowl. When you are done cutting away the segments, give the orange a squeeze to release the remaining juice. Remove the seeds from the segments, if there are any. If you aren't using the juice in your recipe, enjoy it as a "cook's bonus" or stash it in the refrigerator to use later.

BUCKWHEAT FLAPJACKS

with Hibiscus Honey

THE HIBISCUS honey we paired with these tender buckwheat flapjacks has a brilliant ruby color from the hibiscus flowers and a slightly tart flavor that tempers honey's natural sweetness. See the note on page 178 for more about adding flavor to honeys and syrups.

MAKES 8 SERVINGS

5 tsp active dry yeast

5 cups milk, warmed to 110°F

3⅓ cups all-purpose flour

¾ cup buckwheat flour

1 tbsp granulated sugar

1½ tsp salt

4 large egg yolks

4 large egg whites

¼ cup canola oil

½ cup Lemon-Cardamom Butter (page 173)

1½ cups Hibiscus Honey (recipe follows)

1. Dissolve the yeast in the warmed milk and set aside until the yeast foams, 5 to 10 minutes.

2. Sift together the flours, sugar, and salt into a large bowl and make a well in the center of the dry ingredients. Add the egg yolks and yeast mixture to the well and stir until smooth. Cover with plastic wrap and let rise in a warm place until doubled, 1 to 1½ hours.

2. Preheat a gas grill to medium. If you are using a charcoal grill, build a fire and let it burn down until the coals are glowing red with a moderate coating of white ash. Spread the coals in an even bed.

3. Once the batter has risen, beat the egg whites to soft peaks and fold into the batter.

4. Preheat a griddle over direct heat on the grill and lightly grease with some of the oil. Ladle ¼ cup of batter for each flapjack onto the griddle. Turn once, when bubbles break on the upper surface and the bottom is golden brown, about 3 minutes. Finish cooking on the second side, about 2 minutes. Repeat with the remaining batter.

5. Serve the flapjacks on heated plates with the Lemon-Cardamom Butter and the Hibiscus Honey.

LEFT TO RIGHT Flip the pancakes once the bubbles have risen to the surface and started to break and the flapjack is golden brown on the bottom. Steep the honey until it has achieved the color and flavor that you like. Opposite, Buckwheat Flapjacks with warm Hibiscus Honey; warm the syrup slightly before serving to make it easier to pour.

Hibiscus Honey

MAKES 2 CUPS

2 cups honey

1 cup hibiscus flowers

1. Heat the honey to just below the boiling point (185°F) in a double boiler and keep it at that temperature, stirring constantly, about 10 minutes.

2. Remove the honey or syrup from the double boiler and add the hibiscus flowers. Let steep for 1 hour and then strain into a serving bowl or storage container. Store any unused honey in a covered container in the refrigerator for up to 3 weeks.

Flavored Honeys and Syrups

You might be surprised at how many different flavors and qualities of honey there are. Maple syrup, real maple syrup, has a light body and an intense flavor. But, like anything else, there are ways to "gild the lily" for something special.

To make a flavored honey or syrup, first measure out 2 cups and put it in the top of a double boiler. It is important to use a double boiler to keep honeys and syrups from scorching.

Next, add flavorings. We used hibiscus flowers for the honey paired with our buckwheat flapjacks, but there are other options.

Use the following as a guideline, but do taste the syrup or honey as it steeps. Your ingredients may be stronger or weaker in flavor, so let your palate be the ultimate guide. You may want to add more flavoring than suggested below, or perhaps you'll need to shorten or lengthen the steeping time.

- 1 cup hibiscus flowers, steeped for 1 hour
- ¼ cup orange peel, steeped for 45 minutes
- 2 tbsp lemon peel, steeped for 45 minutes
- ½ cup lavender flowers, steeped for 30 minutes
- 2 cinnamon sticks, steeped for 30 minutes
- 1 cup fruit purée (raspberry or blueberry), steeped for 30 minutes
- 2 thick slices ginger, steeped for 30 minutes
- 2 tsp whole cloves, steeped for 15 minutes

Heat the honey or syrup to just below the boiling point (185°F) in a double boiler and keep it at that temperature, stirring constantly, about 10 minutes. Remove the honey or syrup from the double boiler. Add the flavoring of your choice, and let steep according to the times listed above. Strain the honey into a clean serving bowl or storage container.

You can keep flavored syrups and honeys on hand in the refrigerator for up to 3 weeks. Serve flavored honeys and syrups slightly warm to really bring out the aroma.

PEAR SKILLET CAKE

MANY OTHER fruits such as peaches, plums, and pine-apple may also be used in this recipe. When un-molded, this dessert will resemble a tarte Tatin, only with a fraction of the fat and calories.

MAKES 12 SERVINGS

2 cups cake flour

2¼ tsp baking powder

½ tsp baking soda

½ tsp salt

1½ tsp ground ginger

1 tsp ground cinnamon

¼ tsp ground nutmeg

¼ tsp ground mace

¼ tsp ground allspice

2 large Bartlett pears, peeled and cored

2 egg yolks

¼ cup molasses

⅓ cup honey

¼ cup hot water

3 egg whites

2 tbsp butter

½ cup packed light brown sugar

2 cups toasted and/or candied walnut halves
    (see Candied Walnuts, right)

1. Preheat a gas grill to medium-high. Leave one burner off. If you are using a charcoal grill, build a fire and let it burn down until the coals are glowing red with a moderate coating of white ash. Push the coals to one side of the grill. Clean the cooking grate.

2. Sift together the flour, baking powder, baking soda, salt, ginger, cinnamon, nutmeg, mace, and allspice into a medium-sized bowl. Set aside.

3. Grate 1 of the pears. In a small bowl, combine the grated pear, the egg yolks, molasses, and honey, and stir until blended. Add the hot water and stir until the honey and molasses are evenly blended.

4. Stir the wet ingredients into the dry ingredients. In a large bowl, whip the egg whites until stiff peaks form. Fold the egg whites into the batter.

5. Melt the butter in a 10-inch cast-iron skillet on the grill over direct heat. Add the brown sugar and cook until it darkens slightly, about 5 minutes. Remove from heat. Peel, core, and thinly slice the remaining pear. Arrange the pear slices in the skillet in a spiral shape.

6. Pour the batter over the pears in the skillet and place the pan on the grill over indirect heat. Close the lid, and bake until the cake springs back when lightly touched, about 20 minutes.

7. Let the cake cool for 10 minutes and then turn out onto a cake plate. Garnish with the walnuts and serve.

Candied Walnuts

Toast about 1 lb (3 cups) of shelled nuts on an ungreased baking sheet in a 300°F oven until they begin to darken in color and give off a rich, toasted aroma. Stir the nuts once or twice so the nuts on the edges don't overcook before the ones in the center are finished. Immediately transfer the nuts to a metal bowl that you've brushed with butter.

Make the sugar syrup for the nuts: Combine ¾ cup granulated sugar, ½ cup water, and 2 tbsp honey in a saucepan and cook until the mixture reaches the hard-crack stage (300°F). Use a candy thermometer to test the syrup, or pour a small amount into a cup of cold water. The sugar should be easy to snap into pieces once it cools.

Pour the syrup over the nuts, stir with a buttered or oiled spoon, and then spread the mixture on a buttered baking sheet. Once the nuts have cooled, break them into small chunks and store in an airtight container at room temperature for up to 1 month.

HERBED CRÊPES

with Grilled Asparagus and Shallots

Y OU COULD easily fill these crêpes ahead of time. Put the filled crêpes in a lightly oiled baking dish, cover the pan with foil, and refrigerate up to 12 hours before serving. Then, warm them up in a hot oven or right on the grill.

MAKES 8 SERVINGS

¼ cup mustard

1 cup sour cream

¼ cup chopped tarragon

2 bunches asparagus, trimmed and peeled

16 shallots, cut into slices ¼-inch-thick

¼ cup vegetable oil

2 tsp salt

1 tsp ground black pepper

1 cup crumbled goat cheese

16 Herbed Crêpes (recipe follows)

1. Mix together the mustard, sour cream, and tarragon to make a sauce. Refrigerate in a covered container until ready to use (it will last up to 2 days).

2. Preheat a gas grill to medium. If you are using a charcoal grill, build a fire and let it burn down until the coals are glowing red with a moderate coating of white ash. Spread the coals in an even bed. Clean the cooking grate.

3. Brush the asparagus and the shallots lightly with vegetable oil and season with salt and pepper.

4. Place a 5-inch-square piece of foil on the grill. Place the shallots on top of the foil and cook for about 15 minutes, then add the asparagus to the grill. Continue to cook the shallots until tender, about 15 minutes more. Grill the asparagus until tender, about 5 to 7 minutes per side.

5. Spoon 1 tbsp of goat cheese lengthwise in the center of each crêpe. Top each with 4 asparagus spears and 2 tbsp of shallots. Roll up the crêpes. Serve the crêpes on a heated platter or plates, topped with the sauce.

Herbed Crêpes

T O MAKE dessert crêpes with this recipe, substitute 4 tsp sugar for the chopped herbs.

MAKES 16 CRÊPES

2½ cups milk, or more as needed

8 eggs

¼ cup melted butter

2 cups all-purpose flour, or more as needed

1 tsp salt

½ cup chopped herbs of choice (tarragon, parsley, thyme, etc.)

Vegetable oil or cooking spray, as needed

1. Mix together the 2½ cups milk, the eggs, and butter until evenly blended. Add the 2 cups of flour, the salt, and herbs, and stir until smooth. Add a little more milk or flour if necessary to give the batter the consistency of heavy cream. Cover the batter and refrigerate for at least 1 and up to 8 hours.

2. Heat an 8-inch crêpe pan over medium-high heat. Brush it lightly with the oil. Ladle about ¼ cup of the batter into the center of the pan. Tilt the pan to swirl the batter over the surface to the edges.

3. Cook the crêpe until the edges are brown and the underside is golden, about 1 minute. Flip and cook 30 seconds more or until the crêpe is golden brown on both sides. Slide the crêpe onto a plate.

4. Repeat with the remaining batter, stacking the finished crêpes slightly off-center so they will be easier to separate.

SPINACH-FETA OMELET

THE FILLING for this omelet was inspired by spanakopita, a savory Greek pastry filled with spinach and feta cheese. You can substitute frozen spinach that you've defrosted, drained, and chopped for the fresh spinach.

MAKES 8 SERVINGS

6 tbsp canola oil

½ cup minced shallots

4 tsp minced garlic

6 cups spinach leaves, torn into large pieces

1 tbsp salt

1½ tsp ground black pepper

24 large eggs

½ cup milk

1 cup crumbled feta cheese

4 tsp chopped dill

1. Preheat a gas grill to medium-high; leave one burner off. If you are using a charcoal grill, build a fire and let it burn down until the coals are glowing red with a moderate coating of white ash. Spread the coals in an even bed on one side of the grill. Clean the cooking grate.

2. Heat a cast-iron skillet over direct heat on the grill and add 2 tbsp of the oil. Add the shallots and garlic and sauté, stirring frequently, until translucent, about 1 minute.

3. Add the spinach to the pan and sauté, stirring often, until the spinach is just wilted, about 2 minutes. Season the mixture with 1 tsp of the salt and ½ tsp of the pepper. Move the pan to indirect heat to keep warm.

4. Blend the eggs and milk until the yolks and whites are mixed. Season with the remaining salt and pepper.

5. To make each individual omelet: Heat an omelet pan over direct heat and add about 1½ tsp of the oil. Heat until almost smoking, tilting the pan to coat the entire surface of the pan.

6. Pour ½ cup of the beaten eggs into the pan. Swirl the pan on the grill while stirring the eggs in the opposite direction with a heatproof rubber spatula or a wooden spoon. Continue to move the pan and utensil at the same time until the egg mixture has coagulated slightly, about 15 to 20 seconds. Smooth out the eggs into an even layer with a wooden spoon or by shaking the pan.

7. Place 2 tbsp of the feta cheese, ½ tsp of the dill, and about ¼ cup of the spinach mixture lengthwise down the center of the omelet. Let the egg mixture nearly finish cooking without stirring, about 45 seconds to 1 minute.

8. Flip the omelet in half over the filling and slide the omelet onto a plate. Repeat with the remaining ingredients.

SPANISH OMELET

IF YOU have grilled sweet onions or grilled peppers on hand from a previous session at the grill, substitute them for the sautéed peppers and onions called for in this recipe.

MAKES 8 SERVINGS

6 tbsp vegetable oil

2 cups small-dice yellow onion

2 cups small-dice green pepper

4 tsp minced garlic

1 tbsp salt

1½ tsp ground black pepper

24 large eggs

½ cup milk

¼ cup clarified butter or canola oil

1 cup grated manchego cheese

1. Preheat a gas grill to medium-high; leave one burner off. If you are using a charcoal grill, build a fire and let it burn down until the coals are glowing red with a moderate coating of white ash. Spread the coals in an even bed on one side of the grill. Clean the cooking grate.

2. Heat a cast-iron skillet over direct heat on the grill and add 2 tbsp of the oil. Add the onion and green pepper and sauté, stirring frequently, until the onion is translucent, 5 to 6 minutes. Add the garlic to the pan and sauté, stirring often, until the garlic is aromatic, about 1 minute more. Season with 1 tsp of the salt and ½ tsp of the pepper. Move the pan to indirect heat to keep warm.

3. Blend the eggs and milk until the yolks and whites are mixed. Season with the remaining salt and pepper.

4. To make each individual omelet: Heat an omelet pan over direct heat on the grill and add about 1½ tsp of the butter or oil. Heat until almost smoking, tilting the pan to coat the entire surface of the pan.

5. Pour ½ cup of the beaten eggs into the pan. Swirl the pan on the grill while stirring the eggs in the opposite direction with a heatproof rubber spatula or a wooden spoon. Continue to move the pan and stir at the same time until the egg mixture has coagulated slightly, about 15 to 20 seconds. Smooth out the egg into an even layer with a wooden spoon or by shaking the pan.

6. Place about 2 tbsp of the manchego and some of the onion mixture lengthwise down the center of the omelet. Let the egg mixture nearly finish cooking without stirring, about 45 seconds to 1 minute.

7. Flip the omelet in half over the filling and slide the omelet onto a plate. Repeat with the remaining ingredients.

FRIED EGGS

with Mushrooms and Sausage

THE MUSHROOMS and onions are a great topping for this breakfast dish, but they are not essential. If you like, griddle some hard rolls or bagels and make a sandwich from this classic combination.

MAKES 8 SERVINGS

½ cup canola oil

¾ pound mushrooms, thinly sliced

4 cups thin-sliced yellow onions

1 tbsp salt, or to taste

2 tsp ground black pepper, or to taste

¾ pound breakfast sausage

16 large eggs

1. Preheat a gas grill to medium-high; leave one burner off. If you are using a charcoal grill, build a fire and let it burn down until the coals are glowing red with a moderate coating of white ash. Spread the coals in an even bed on one side of the grill. Clean the cooking grate.

2. Heat 2 tbsp of the oil in a pan over direct heat on the grill until almost smoking. Add the mushrooms and sauté, stirring occasionally, until lightly caramelized, 5 to 6 minutes. Remove the mushrooms from the pan and set aside.

3. Add another 2 tbsp of the oil to the pan over direct heat. Add the onions and sauté until lightly browned, about 5 to 7 minutes. Return the mushrooms to the pan and season with about 1 tsp salt and ½ tsp of pepper, or to taste. Move the pan to indirect heat to keep warm.

4. Divide the sausage into 8 equal portions and shape into patties. Heat a cast-iron skillet over direct heat on the grill. Add the sausage patties and fry until golden brown and cooked thoroughly, 3 to 5 minutes on each side. Drain on paper towels and keep warm.

5. Wipe out the skillet you used to cook the sausage and place over direct heat on the grill. Add the remaining oil to the pan. Heat the oil until hot but not smoking, tilting the pan to coat the entire surface of the pan. Crack the eggs directly into the hot pan and immediately move the pan to indirect heat to finish frying them. Fry the eggs, shaking the pan occasionally to keep the eggs from sticking. Season the eggs with salt and pepper. Fry for about 2 minutes for sunny-side-up eggs, 3 minutes for medium yolks, and 3½ to 4 minutes for hard yolks.

6. Serve the fried eggs at once topped with some of the mushroom mixture and a sausage patty.

TOAD IN A HOLE

with Red Pepper Ketchup

THIS IS only as good as the ingredients that you put in it. If you use really flavorful artisan bread, the whole dish will taste better. You may serve one or two pieces, depending on your guests' appetite.

MAKES 8 SERVINGS

16 slices sourdough bread, about ¾ inch thick

1 cup melted butter, or as needed

16 eggs

2 tsp salt, or to taste

1 tsp ground black pepper, or to taste

1 cup Red Pepper Ketchup (recipe follows)

1. Preheat a gas grill to medium-high; leave one burner off. If you are using a charcoal grill, build a fire and let it burn down until the coals are glowing red with a moderate coating of white ash. Spread the coals in an even bed on one side of the grill. Clean the cooking grate.

2. Cut holes in the center of each slice of bread using a 2½-inch biscuit cutter. Be sure not to get too close to the crust of the bread. Brush both sides of each slice of bread with the melted butter.

3. Heat a griddle to medium over direct heat on the grill. Griddle the bread on 1 side until golden brown, about 1 to 2 minutes. Flip each piece of bread over and crack 1 egg into the hole in each piece of bread.

4. Move the pan to indirect heat. Season the eggs with salt and pepper. Fry the eggs for about 2 minutes for sunny-side-up eggs, 3 minutes for medium yolks, and 3½ to 4 minutes for hard yolks. Flip the bread over, being careful not to break the yolk, and cook for 30 seconds more, if desired.

5. Serve immediately with the Red Pepper Ketchup on top or on the side.

Red Pepper Ketchup

MAKES 2 CUPS

¼ cup olive oil

5 red peppers, diced

2 tbsp minced shallots

¾ cup dry white wine

¾ cup chicken or vegetable broth

1 tsp salt

½ tsp ground black pepper

1. Heat the olive oil in a large sauté pan over medium heat. Add the peppers and shallots and sauté until tender, about 5 to 6 minutes.

2. Deglaze the pan with the white wine, making sure to scrape up anything that is stuck to the bottom of the pan.

3. Add the broth and simmer until reduced to half the original volume. Allow the mixture to cool to room temperature.

4. Purée the mixture until smooth. Season the ketchup with the salt and pepper.

CORNMEAL-CRUSTED TROUT

BUTTERFLYING WHOLE trout makes it easier to cook and more convenient to eat.

MAKES 8 SERVINGS

8 thick slices bacon, diced small

8 brook trout, butterflied

1 tbsp salt

1 tsp ground black pepper

3 cups cornmeal

Canola oil, as needed

Fried parsley (see note at right)

2 lemons, cut into wedges

1. Preheat a gas grill to medium-high; leave one burner off. If you are using a charcoal grill, build a fire and let it burn down until the coals are glowing red with a moderate coating of white ash. Spread the coals in an even bed on one side of the grill. Clean the cooking grate.

2. Preheat a large cast-iron skillet over direct heat on the grill until hot. Add the bacon and cook, stirring, until crisp, about 2 to 3 minutes. Remove the bacon with a slotted spoon and set aside on paper towels to drain. Reserve the skillet with the bacon drippings.

3. Season the trout with the salt and pepper and dredge in the cornmeal.

4. Return the bacon fat in the skillet to direct heat on the grill and add enough of the oil to come to a depth of ¼ inch.

5. Heat the oil until the surface ripples; it should not be smoking, however. Add the trout, working in batches to avoid overcrowding the pan. Pan-fry until golden brown on both sides, about 3 to 4 minutes per side. Carefully slide the pan to indirect heat if needed to prevent scorching.

6. Serve the trout immediately on heated plates, garnished with the reserved bacon, fried parsley, and lemon wedges.

Fried Parsley

Fried parsley is a traditional garnish for pan-fried fish. To prepare it, select attractive sprigs of parsley, clean them well in cool water, and spin dry completely. Heat enough canola oil to fill a small saucepan to a ½-inch depth. Add the sprigs a few at a time. They should be completely submerged in oil. Fry, stirring gently, until translucent and crisp, about 30 to 45 seconds. Remove the sprigs with a slotted spoon and drain on paper towels. Continue until all of the parsley is fried. It will keep at room temperature, uncovered, up to 4 hours.

LEFT TO RIGHT Dredge the fish lightly inside and out with cornmeal. Be sure not to overcrowd the pan and be careful when flipping the fish so that the oil doesn't splash. You can serve the fish whole or cut them into 2 fillets when it is time to eat. Opposite, the Cornmeal-crusted Trout, garnished with lemon wedges and fried parsley.

GRILLED FLANK STEAK HASH

USE WHATEVER grilled meat you have on hand for this hash. Even grilled or poached fish is delicious. Make the hash ahead of time and store it already shaped for a quicker start to the day. Top the hash with scrambled eggs, if you wish.

MAKES 8 SERVINGS

2¼ lb grilled flank steak, diced small

2½ cups peeled, diced potatoes

1½ cups diced yellow onions

1 cup diced celery

½ cup diced green beans (blanched and cooled before dicing)

½ cup minced mushrooms

¼ cup vegetable oil

½ tsp salt

¼ tsp ground black pepper

1. Preheat a gas grill to medium-high; leave one burner off. If you are using a charcoal grill, build a fire and let it burn down until the coals are glowing red with a moderate coating of white ash. Spread the coals in an even layer on one side of the grill. Clean the cooking grate.

2. Combine the flank steak, potatoes, onions, celery, green beans, and mushrooms in a large bowl. Drizzle 2 tbsp oil over the mixture, add the salt and pepper, and toss to coat evenly.

3. Grind the mixture through a meat grinder or chop into a coarse paste with a chef's knife. Form into 16 patties.

4. Brush the patties with the remaining oil and grill over direct heat until crisp on the first side, about 2 minutes. Turn the patties over and move them to indirect heat. Continue to grill, covered, until the hash is crisp and cooked through, turning as necessary, about 10 minutes more.

5. Serve the hash immediately on a heated platter or individual plates.

GRILLED HAM STEAKS

with Grilled Pineapple Salsa

COUNTRY HAM can be very salty. To remove some of the salt, blanch the ham steaks by placing them in a skillet with enough cold water to cover generously. Bring to a simmer over low heat, simmer for 2 or 3 minutes, then drain and pat the steaks dry before continuing with the recipe.

MAKES 8 SERVINGS

8 ham steaks, ¼ inch thick

¼ cup canola oil, or as needed

¾ tsp ground black pepper

1 cup Grilled Pineapple Salsa (recipe follows)

1. Preheat a gas grill to medium. If you are using a charcoal grill, build a fire and let it burn down until the coals are glowing red with a moderate coating of white ash. Spread the coals in an even bed. Clean the cooking grate.

2. Brush the ham steaks with the canola oil and season with the pepper.

3. Grill the ham steaks on 1 side until marked, about 4 minutes. Flip the ham steaks over and grill for 2 to 3 minutes, or until cooked through and deep golden brown on both sides.

4. Spoon 2 tbsp of the salsa over each ham steak and serve immediately.

Grilled Pineapple Salsa

A TOUCH OF basil, along with freshly grilled pineapple, gives a unique twist to this flavorful salsa.

MAKES 2 CUPS

½ pineapple, sliced ¼ inch thick

½ red onion, sliced ¼ inch thick

1 jalapeño

5 tbsp peanut oil

1½ tsp salt, or to taste

¾ tsp ground black pepper, or to taste

3 tbsp lime juice

¾ tsp grated lime zest

3 tbsp chopped basil

1. Preheat a gas grill to medium. If you are using a charcoal grill, build a fire and let it burn down until the coals are glowing red with a moderate coating of white ash. Spread the coals in an even bed. Clean the cooking grate.

2. Brush the pineapple, onion, and the jalapeño with about 2 tbsp of the oil and season with ½ tsp of the salt and ¼ tsp of the pepper. Grill over direct heat until well marked and tender, about 2 to 3 minutes per side for the pineapple, 4 minutes per side for the onion, and 2 to 3 minutes per side for the jalapeño. Remove from the grill and let cool.

3. Cut the pineapple and the onions into a small dice. Mince the jalapeño. Combine the pineapple, onion, and jalapeño with the remaining peanut oil, the lime juice, lime zest, and basil. Season with the remaining salt and pepper.

4. Allow the mixture to stand for 1 hour before using. Store any unused salsa in a covered container in the refrigerator for up to 4 days.

GRILLED SKIRT STEAK

with Jalapeño-Cilantro Butter

I F YOU can find skirt steak, it is a great match for the gutsy flavors of this green-flecked butter. Serve the steaks with biscuits or cornbread and plenty of campfire coffee.

MAKES 8 SERVINGS

4 tbsp softened unsalted butter

2 tbsp minced fresh cilantro

1 tbsp finely minced jalapeño

Grated zest of ½ lime

Salt and freshly ground pepper

4 skirt steaks (about 8 oz each)

Vegetable oil for brushing

1. For the Jalapeño-Cilantro Butter, blend the butter with the cilantro, jalapeño, lime zest, ¼ tsp salt, and ¼ tsp pepper. Taste and adjust the seasoning. Transfer the butter onto a piece of plastic wrap. Roll into a 1-inch-diameter cylinder and secure the ends by twisting. Transfer to the refrigerator and chill until firm, about 2 hours. *(See Flavored Butters, page 119)*

2. Preheat a gas grill to medium-high, leaving one burner off. If you are using a charcoal grill, build a fire and let it burn down until the coals are glowing red with a moderate coating of white ash. Spread the coals in an even bed on one side of the grill. Clean the cooking grate.

3. Season the steaks with salt and pepper and brush them lightly with oil. Grill the steaks on the first side until marked, about 3 minutes. Turn the steaks over and continue cooking until the meat registers 145°F for medium-rare, 3 to 4 minutes more. If you prefer beef done medium, move the steaks to the cooler grill zone and cook for 5 to 6 minutes more.

4. Cut the steaks into portions and top each portion with a slice of the flavored butter and serve at once.

DESSERTS

ESSERTS FROM THE grill might seem revolutionary, but if you've ever enjoyed a toasted marshmallow sandwiched with graham crackers and chocolate, then you've made dessert over an open fire. We've included fresh fruits, skewered or sliced, and grilled just long enough to get a touch of the grill's intense flavor and paired them with cooling ice creams, ice milks, and sorbets. Cakes—pound cake and angel food cake—are great from the grill too.

It is always important to clean your grill before you put foods down on it to cook, but it is especially important when you are grilling sweet foods like fruits or cakes. Skewers and hand racks help you turn your grilled desserts more easily. Most grilled desserts aren't on the fire for very long, so a brisk, hot fire is best. A little smoke and charring is great, but with all the sugar in sweet foods, you need to keep a watchful eye to avoid blackening them to the point of bitterness.

BROWNIES

with Grilled Fruit Salsa

F UDGE BROWNIES pair well with the sweet-tart tastes of this grilled fruit salsa. These brownies freeze very well, so make a double batch to have on hand.

MAKES 8 SERVINGS

½ papaya, peeled and cut into ¼-inch-thick slices

1 mango, peeled and cut into ¼-inch-thick slices

¼ honeydew melon, peeled and cut into ¼-inch-thick slices

6 strawberries, hulled and diced small

2 tbsp passion fruit juice

1 tbsp fine-chopped mint

⅓ cup amaretto liqueur

1 cup orange juice

½ cup granulated sugar

8 Brownies (recipe follows)

1. Preheat a gas grill to medium-high. If you are using a charcoal grill, build a fire and let it burn down until the coals are glowing red with a light coating of white ash. Spread the coals in an even bed. Clean the cooking grate.

2. Grill the papaya, mango, and honeydew over direct heat until well marked on both sides, about 1 to 2 minutes per side for the mango and papaya and 1 minute for the honeydew. Remove from the grill and let cool to room temperature.

3. Cut the grilled fruit slices into a ¼-inch dice. Combine the grilled fruit, strawberries, passion fruit juice, and mint. Refrigerate in a covered container for at least 1 and up to 8 hours to allow the flavors to develop.

4. Combine the amaretto, orange juice, and sugar in a saucepan and bring to a boil. Boil until reduced by half, about 30 minutes. Allow the mixture to cool to room temperature.

5. Gently stir together the reduced liquid and the fruit mix-

ture. Serve the salsa over the brownies, or store in a covered container in the refrigerator for up to 2 days.

Brownies

MAKES 16 BARS

1⅔ cup butter

2 cups chopped unsweetened chocolate

6 large eggs

3⅔ cups granulated sugar

2 tsp vanilla extract

¼ tsp salt

⅓ cup cake flour, sifted

2 cups coarse-chopped toasted pecans

1. Preheat oven to 350°F. Line a baking pan (13 × 9 × 2 inches) with parchment paper, making sure the paper comes up the sides of the pan.

2. Melt the butter and chocolate in a metal bowl over a pan of simmering water, blending gently (or use a double boiler). Remove from heat.

3. Whip the eggs, sugar, vanilla, and salt on high speed until thick and light in color, about 8 minutes. Blend ⅓ of the egg mixture into the melted chocolate, then return it to the remaining egg mixture and blend on medium seed, scraping the bowl as needed.

4. Mix in the flour and nuts on low speed until just blended. The batter will be very wet. Pour the batter into the prepared pan and spread out evenly.

5. Bake the brownies until a crust forms but they are still moist in the center, about 45 to 50 minutes. Let cool completely in the pan. Cut into 16 bars.

BANANAS FOSTER TARTLETS

BANANAS FOSTER is a classic, and dramatic, tableside dessert. We've grilled the bananas instead of flambéing them here and present them over pastry cream in a pastry case, instead of serving them over ice cream.

MAKES 8 SERVINGS

1-2-3 Dough (recipe follows)

½ cup Pastry Cream (recipe follows)

¼ cup heavy cream

6 tbsp butter

¼ cup granulated sugar

1 tsp lemon juice

6 tbsp dark or light rum

2 tbsp banana liqueur

3 bananas

¼ cup chopped toasted macadamia nuts

1. On a lightly floured surface, roll the dough out to ⅛-inch thickness. Cut eight 4-inch rounds out of the dough, and line 8 greased 3-inch tartlet pans with the dough. (If you cannot get 8 rounds after rolling out the dough the first time, gather up the scraps, re-roll the dough to ⅛-inch thickness, and cut out the needed rounds.) Trim any excess dough from the tartlet pans.

2. Line the dough with 4-inch squares of parchment paper and fill the bottom of the tartlet pans with dried beans or pie weights. Chill the dough for 10 minutes in the refrigerator before baking.

3. Preheat oven to 350°F.

4. Bake the tartlets for 12 minutes, or until par baked. Remove the beans and the parchment paper and return the tartlet shells to the oven for 5 minutes, or until the shells are golden brown. Allow the shells to cool to room temperature.

5. Whip the pastry cream until smooth if it has been refrigerated. Whip the heavy cream to soft peaks. Combine the pastry cream and whipped cream, and spoon the mixture into the tartlet shells, filling each ¾ full. Refrigerate the shells, covered, until ready to use. *(recipe continues on page 198)*

LEFT TO RIGHT Carefully shingle the bananas on top of the pastry cream; it may be necessary to use a palette knife or small butter knife to place the bananas, as they will be soft. Spoon the sauce over the tartlets while they are still on the parchment paper just in case it drips. Serve these immediately after assembling them, to take advantage of the contrast between the hot bananas and the cold pastry cream.

6. Heat the butter in a medium-sized skillet over medium-high heat. Add the sugar and cook until the sugar has started to darken slightly. Add the lemon juice and swirl it into the butter mixture.

7. Remove the pan from the heat, and pour in the rum and the banana liqueur. Return the pan to the heat and bring to a simmer. (If desired, you can "flame" the rum with a match. This is not essential, however.) Keep the sauce warm.

8. Preheat a gas grill to high. If you are using a charcoal grill, build a fire and let it burn down until the coals are glowing red with a light coating of white ash. Spread the coals in an even bed.

9. Peel the bananas and cut into rounds or on the diagonal about ½ inch thick.

10. Grill the bananas until just softened, about 1 to 2 minutes, basting with the sauce once.

11. Cut the bananas in half so that each slice is ¼ inch thick. Divide the bananas evenly among the tartlet shells, shingling the bananas, if desired. Drizzle the remaining sauce over the bananas. Garnish with the toasted macadamia nuts and serve immediately.

1-2-3 Dough

MAKES ENOUGH FOR 8 TARTLETS

1 cup softened butter

½ cup granulated sugar

¾ tsp vanilla extract

1 egg

½ tsp grated lemon zest

3 cups all-purpose flour

1. Cream together the butter, sugar, and vanilla extract by hand or on medium speed using the paddle attachment of an electric mixer until very light and fluffy, about 5 minutes.

2. Add the egg and beat until fully incorporated, scraping down the sides as necessary.

3. Add the lemon zest and flour, and mix until just incorporated.

4. Shape the dough into a disk and chill in the refrigerator for 1 hour before using.

Pastry Cream

YOU'LL HAVE better control over this pastry cream as it cooks, with less danger of scorching, if you make the full batch. Any pastry cream you don't use can be kept in the refrigerator for up to 5 days. You can make it into a quick dessert by folding in some whipped cream and serving it as a mousse or pudding.

MAKES 4 CUPS

4 cups milk

1 cup granulated sugar

⅔ cup cornstarch

6 eggs

1 tbsp vanilla extract

6 tbsp butter

1. Combine the milk with half the sugar in a saucepan and bring to a boil.

2. Combine the remaining sugar with the cornstarch, add the eggs, and mix until smooth.

3. Temper the egg mixture (see note opposite) into the hot milk and bring to a full boil, stirring constantly.

4. Remove from the heat and stir in the vanilla and butter. Transfer to a clean container, place a piece of plastic wrap directly on top the pastry cream, and let cool. Store any unused cream in a covered container in the refrigerator; let cool thoroughly before storing.

CRÊPES

with Grilled Pears and Butterscotch Sauce

SELECT PEARS that are ripe but still firm for this dish; Anjou or Bosc are good choices and readily available.

MAKES 8 SERVINGS

1 cup dried cherries

1 cup pear nectar

1 cup rough-chopped toasted pecans

1 cup heavy cream

4 medium pears, cored and cut into ½-inch-thick slices

2 tbsp lemon juice

1 tbsp granulated sugar

16 Crêpes (page 181)

1 cup Butterscotch Sauce (page 203)

1. Preheat a gas grill to high. If you are using a charcoal grill, build a fire and let it burn down until the coals are glowing red with a light coating of white ash. Spread the coals in an even bed. Clean the cooking grate.

2. Bring the cherries and the pear nectar to a simmer in a saucepan over medium heat. As soon as the nectar is simmering, remove it from the heat, cover, and let steep for 10 minutes. Stir in ½ cup of the pecans.

3. Whip the heavy cream to soft peaks. Refrigerate until ready to serve.

4. Toss the pears with the lemon juice and sugar.

5. Grill the pears over direct heat until tender in the middle and well marked, 2 to 3 minutes per side.

6. Spoon some of the cherry mixture lengthwise down the center of each crêpe. Divide the grilled pears among the crêpes. Roll up the crêpes.

7. Serve the crêpes topped with the Butterscotch Sauce, the whipped cream, and the remaining pecans.

Tempering

Pastry cream and the custard base for ice creams rely upon a specific technique, known as tempering. These recipes include a significant amount of eggs. Tempering means that you slowly increase the heat of the eggs before adding them to the hot milk or cream. Then, they can be added without scrambling or curdling in the pan. To temper eggs into a hot liquid, follow these steps:

1. Bring the liquid (milk, cream, or a mixture of both) to a simmer, along with any flavorings you want to include (see page 200 for more about flavoring ice creams), and some of the sugar.

2. Meanwhile, blend the eggs and remaining sugar until smooth. Pastry cream always includes a thickener; our recipe calls for cornstarch.

To break up the cornstarch, stir it together with the sugar before you add the sugar to the eggs. Blend until smooth.

3. Once the milk or cream reaches a simmer, remove the pan from the heat. Ladle a small amount of the hot milk into the egg mixture, stirring as you add it. Continue adding the hot milk or cream until you've blended about ⅓ of it into the egg mixture. The eggs are tempered at this point.

4. Now, pour the egg mixture back into the pan with the rest of the hot milk or cream and stir.

5. Return the pan to low heat and carefully heat the pastry cream or custard sauce, stirring constantly with a wooden spoon.

GRILLED BANANA SPLIT

with Homemade Ice Cream

CHOOSE FIRM-RIPE bananas for this dish. The heat of the grill will intensify the bananas' natural sweetness. Fully ripe and soft bananas won't hold up to the intense heat of the grill.

MAKES 6 SERVINGS

6 bananas, peeled and cut in half

2 tbsp melted butter

3 cups ice cream: French Vanilla, Dark or White Chocolate, Cherry Vanilla, and/or Praline Ice Cream (page 202)

2 cups sauce: Chocolate, Cherry, and/or Butterscotch Sauce (page 203)

½ cup coarsely chopped toasted almonds

1 cup whipped cream

6 brandied or maraschino cherries

1. Preheat a gas grill to low. If you are using a charcoal grill, build a fire and let it burn down until the coals have a heavy coating of white ash. Spread the coals in an even bed. Clean the cooking grate.

2. Brush the bananas with the melted butter and place on the grill. Grill the bananas until lightly marked on the first side, about 1 minute. Turn the bananas carefully and grill on the second side until lightly marked and hot, 1 minute more.

3. Place 2 banana halves on each serving plate. Top each serving with 3 small scoops of the ice cream and spoon the sauces over the ice cream. Garnish with the whipped cream, toasted almonds, and cherries.

Making Ice Cream

Ice cream is the perfect ending to grilled meals and a perfect foil for grilled fruits. You can certainly use good-quality purchased brands of ice cream, but with an ice cream freezer and a little planning, you can have a fresh batch of ice cream ready to serve in a very short time.

The basic French Vanilla Ice Cream recipe is made from essentially the same ingredients as a custard. Making variations is simple. You have three basic options to flavor an ice cream made from a custard base, like this one:

ADD A FLAVORING TO THE MILK AND CREAM AS IT HEATS

Things like vanilla beans, whole spices, coarsely ground coffee, or tea are the ingredients you want to steep into the ice cream. Then, they are strained out before you freeze the ice cream.

STIR A FLAVORING INTO THE ICE CREAM'S CUSTARD BASE, BEFORE YOU FREEZE THE ICE CREAM

Melted chocolate and fruit purées are examples of some flavorings you might add this way. To keep the flavor of fruit purées fresh, stir them into a chilled custard base.

STIR OR FOLD "ADD-INS" AND RIPPLES AFTER THE ICE CREAM HAS FROZEN BUT BEFORE TRANSFERRING IT TO THE FREEZER

Add-ins like chopped nuts, diced or whole fruit pieces, chocolate pieces, crushed cookies, or candy bars are folded in until they are evenly mixed throughout. Ripples—fudge, caramel, or butterscotch, for instance—are just folded into the ice cream until they are streaked throughout the batch.

French Vanilla Ice Cream

THIS BASIC ice cream can be flavored to suit your mood or the bounty of the farmer's market. See the suggestions following this recipe, but don't limit yourself to what we've included here. Try peaches, pistachios, caramel sauce, chocolate chunks, or crushed cookies to create your own specialty of the house.

MAKES 4 CUPS

2 cups heavy cream
½ cup granulated sugar
⅛ tsp salt
1 vanilla bean, split, or 2 tsp vanilla extract
6 large egg yolks

1. Combine the cream, ¼ cup of the sugar, and the salt in a heavy-gauge pan over medium heat and bring to a simmer. If you are using a split vanilla bean, add it to the cream as it comes to a simmer. Remove the pan from the heat as soon as it reaches a simmer.

2. Blend the egg yolks with the remaining ¼ cup sugar until smooth and light. Ladle about half of the hot cream mixture into the blended yolks, adding it a little at a time and whisking constantly as you work. (See tempering note on page 199.)

3. Pour the yolk mixture into the cream and return the pan to low heat. Cook, stirring constantly with a wooden spoon, until thickened enough to cling to the back of the spoon. (Do not bring to a full boil.)

4. Strain the mixture through a fine-mesh sieve into a clean container set in a bowl of ice water. If you are using vanilla extract, stir it into the mixture now. Continue to stir until the ice cream base has cooled to 70°F. Cover the container, refrigerate for at least 12 hours.

5. Set up your ice cream freezer according to the manufacturer's directions, add the ice cream base, and freeze until it is very thick but still soft enough to stir.

6. Transfer the ice cream to a freezer container and place in the freezer to firm and ripen for at least 4 hours before serving.

Dark or White Chocolate Ice Cream

Add 1 cup of milk to the cream before bringing it to a simmer. Strain the ice cream base over ⅔ cup finely chopped dark or white chocolate, and stir the mixture until the chocolate has melted and is well blended. Place the bowl over an ice bath and stir until cooled properly.

Cherry Vanilla Ice Cream

Omit the vanilla bean. Add 1½ tsp almond extract to the ice cream before you put it in the ice cream freezer. Fold 1 cup pitted sweet or sour cherries into the ice cream when you take it out of the ice cream freezer, before putting it into the freezer to firm and ripen.

Praline Ice Cream

Substitute brown sugar for the granulated sugar. Add 2 tbsp praline paste (available in some specialty shops or through mail-order sources) to the milk and cream as the mixture comes to a simmer. Fold 1 cup coarse-chopped toasted hazelnuts into the ice cream when you take it out of the ice cream freezer, before putting it into the freezer to firm and ripen.

Hot Chocolate Sauce

MAKES 2 CUPS

2 cups fine-chopped bittersweet chocolate

1 cup heavy cream

2 tsp vanilla extract

1. Place the chocolate in a stainless-steel bowl.

2. Bring the cream just to a simmer and pour it over the chocolate. Add the vanilla and whisk until smooth.

3. Serve the sauce now, or let cool and store in a covered container in the refrigerator for up to 10 days. Reheat in a microwave on low power or in a double boiler.

Cherry Sauce

MAKES 2 CUPS

1¼ lb pitted Bing cherries (about 3¾ cups)

2½ cups granulated sugar

¾ cup water

¼ tsp almond extract

1½ tsp lemon juice, or to taste

1. Combine the cherries, sugar, and water in a saucepan, crushing the cherries slightly with the back of a wooden spoon to release some of their juices. Bring to a simmer over medium heat. Remove from the heat, cover, and let the cherries steep for 1 hour.

2. Add the water and almond extract. Return the pan to medium heat and bring to a simmer. Reduce the heat to low and continue to simmer the sauce until the juices thicken, about 30 minutes.

3. Add the lemon juice. (Optional: Let the sauce cool slightly and then purée the sauce in a blender for a smooth sauce.)

4. Serve the sauce now, or let cool and store in a covered container in the refrigerator for up to 10 days. Reheat in a microwave on low power or in a double boiler.

Butterscotch Sauce

MAKES 2 CUPS

1⅓ cups packed dark brown sugar

¾ cup light corn syrup

½ cup butter

2 tbsp water

Pinch salt

½ cup heavy cream

1. Combine the brown sugar, syrup, butter, water and salt in a heavy saucepan and bring to a boil over medium heat, stirring constantly. Boil for 2 minutes.

2. Remove the pan from the heat, let cool slightly, and stir in the cream.

3. Serve the sauce now, or let cool and store in a covered container in the refrigerator for up to 10 days. Reheat in a microwave on low power or in a double boiler.

GRILLED FRUIT SKEWERS

with Buttermilk Ice Milk

BUTTERMILK GIVES the ice milk served with these fruit skewers a delicious tang. It's the perfect foil for tropical fruits like bananas, pineapples, mangos, and papayas. When these fruits aren't in season, substitute other fruits like tree-ripened peaches, plums, nectarines, and apricots.

MAKES 8 SERVINGS

8 bamboo skewers, 10 inches long

2 mangos, peeled and seeded

2 small papayas, peeled and seeded

¼ pineapple, peeled and cored

8 strawberries

Buttermilk Ice Milk (recipe follows)

1. Soak the skewers in cool water for 30 minutes.

2. Preheat a gas grill to medium. If you are using a charcoal grill, build a fire and let it burn down until the coals are glowing red with a moderate coating of white ash. Spread the coals in an even bed. Clean the cooking grate.

3. Cut the fruits into relatively equal-sized pieces. Thread the fruit onto the skewers, alternating them. Grill the fruit skewers, turning as necessary, until slightly charred and hot, about 6 to 8 minutes, depending on the ripeness of the fruit.

4. Serve the fruit skewers with the Buttermilk Ice Milk.

Buttermilk Ice Milk

AN ICE milk is lower in fat than a traditional custard-based ice cream, but adding a bit of heavy cream gives this ice milk a noticeable richness.

MAKES 8 SERVINGS

3 cups milk

1 cup heavy cream

1 cup plus 2 tbsp granulated sugar

¼ tsp salt

1¼ cups egg yolks

1 tbsp vanilla extract

1 cup buttermilk

1. Heat the milk, heavy cream, ½ cup of the sugar, and the salt in a saucepan over medium heat until the mixture just reaches a boil. Remove from the heat.

2. Whisk together the egg yolks and the remaining sugar. Temper the egg mixture (see tempering note on page 199) by gradually adding about one-half of the hot milk mixture into the egg mixture, whipping constantly. Add the tempered egg mixture to the remaining hot milk in the saucepan and whisk to combine.

3. Return the saucepan to the heat and cook, stirring constantly, until the mixture thickens enough to evenly coat the back of a spoon (180°F), about 2 to 3 minutes.

4. Stir in the vanilla extract. Strain the mixture into a metal container and immediately transfer to an ice bath. Cool to below 40°F. Cover and refrigerate the mixture for at least 8 and up to 12 hours.

5. Stir the buttermilk into the chilled base. Process the mixture in an ice cream machine according to the manufacturer's instructions. Transfer the ice milk from the machine to storage containers, and pack it tightly. Cover and freeze for several hours or overnight before serving.

GRILLED PEACHES

with Vanilla Ice Cream and Raspberry Sauce

THIS DESSERT echoes the flavors of a classic dessert, peach Melba.

MAKES 8 SERVINGS

4 peaches, cut into ½-inch-thick slices

¼ cup granulated sugar

2 tbsp lemon juice

4 cups French Vanilla Ice Cream (see page 202)

1 cup Raspberry Sauce (recipe follows)

8 Citrus Crisps (recipe follows)

1. Preheat a gas grill to high. If you are using a charcoal grill, build a fire and let it burn down until the coals are glowing red with a light coating of white ash. Spread the coals in an even bed. Clean the cooking grate.

2. Toss the peaches with the sugar and lemon juice.

3. Grill the peaches over direct heat until tender in the middle and well marked, 2 to 3 minutes per side

4. Serve the peaches over the French Vanilla Ice Cream, topped with the Raspberry Sauce and garnished with the Citrus Crisps.

Raspberry Sauce

MAKES 2 CUPS

1 lb raspberries, fresh or frozen

½ cup granulated sugar, or more to taste

1 tbsp lemon juice, or more to taste

1. Combine the raspberries, sugar, and lemon juice in a saucepan over medium heat. Simmer, stirring, until the sugar has dissolved, about 10 minutes.

2. Strain the sauce through a fine-mesh sieve. Add additional sugar and/or lemon juice to taste, if desired.

3. Serve now, or store in a covered container in the refrigerator for up to 7 days.

Citrus Crisps

MAKES 24 COOKIES

1 cup softened butter

½ cup granulated sugar

½ tsp salt

½ tsp vanilla extract

1½ cups quick-cooking rolled oats

1 cup all-purpose flour, sifted

½ cup grated lemon zest

1. Preheat oven to 350°F. Line 2 baking sheets with parchment paper or silicone baking mats.

2. Cream together the butter, sugar, salt, and vanilla extract by hand or using the paddle attachment of an electric mixer until very smooth and light, about 3 minutes.

3. Add the oats, flour, and lemon zest, and mix on low speed until just combined, scraping down the bowl as necessary to blend evenly.

4. Form the dough into 1-inch balls (about 1 tbsp of dough per ball) and place in even rows approximately 2 inches apart on the prepared sheet pans. Flatten slightly with the palm of your hand.

5. Bake until the edges are light golden brown, about 12 to 15 minutes. Transfer to wire racks and let cool completely before serving or storing in airtight containers.

BAKED APPLES

Filled with Walnuts and Cream

THESE BAKED apples are perfect for a cookout in the fall. They are the kind of dessert you'd want to put on the grill when you just take off your entrée. By the time you've eaten and brewed coffee, the apples are ready to eat, and the smell is wonderful. If you can't find Calvados, substitute cognac or brandy.

MAKES 8 SERVINGS

2 tbsp chopped toasted walnuts

2 tbsp packed light brown sugar

2 tbsp softened butter

8 prunes, pitted and diced small

½ tsp grated lemon zest

8 McIntosh apples, cored

2 tbsp Calvados

3 tbsp maple syrup, grade B

½ cup heavy cream

1. Preheat a gas grill to medium. If you are using a charcoal grill, build a fire and let it burn down until the coals are glowing red with a moderate coating of white ash. Spread the coals in an even bed. Clean the cooking grate.

2. Combine the walnuts, brown sugar, butter, prunes, and lemon zest, and mix until evenly blended. Pack the mixture into the cored apples.

3. Cut 8 large rectangles of foil and fold each in half to make squares. Set 1 filled apple in the center of each square. Drizzle each apple with some of the calvados (less than 1 tsp per apple) and a little of the maple syrup (less than 1 tsp per apple). Pull up the sides of the foil around the apple to make a vented pouch.

4. Grill the apples over direct heat until soft and the juices that collect in the bottom of the pouch are a rich brown, about 35 to 40 minutes. Turn the pouches occasionally as the apples cook.

5. Whip the heavy cream just until lightly thickened and still somewhat runny. Whisk in the remaining maple syrup.

6. To serve, place a baked apple on each serving dish. Pour the accumulated juices from the foil pouches over the grilled apples, then spoon some of the whipped cream over them. Serve immediately.

Pick up a variety of apples from your local farmer's market once the season starts and try them out, to see which one is your favorite to use in this dessert.

GRILLED PEPPERED PINEAPPLE

with Tequila–Orange Sauce and Candied Kumquats

IF YOU can't find kumquats in the store, cut the peel of two oranges into thin strips and use that in place of the halved kumquats called for in the Candied Kumquat recipe.

MAKES 8 SERVINGS

3 cups orange juice

1 cup silver tequila

½ cup honey

1 large pineapple, cut into ½-inch-thick rings

1 tbsp brine-packed green peppercorns, rinsed well

2 cups French Vanilla Ice Cream (see page 202)

¾ cup Candied Kumquats (recipe follows)

1. Combine the orange juice, tequila, and honey in a small, heavy saucepan. Simmer over medium heat until reduced to about 1 cup, about 45 to 50 minutes. The sauce will appear slightly thick and syrupy. Keep warm. (If the sauce is made in advance, let the sauce cool and store in a covered container in the refrigerator for up to 5 days. Warm the sauce before serving.)

2. Preheat a gas grill to high. If you are using a charcoal grill, build a fire and let it burn down until the coals are glowing red with a light coating of white ash. Spread the coals in an even bed. Clean the cooking grate.

3. Rub both sides of the pineapple rings with the peppercorns. Grill over direct heat, turning as necessary, until both sides are well caramelized, about 6 to 8 minutes.

4. Serve the grilled pineapple on dessert plates, drizzled with the tequila-orange sauce and topped with a ¼-cup scoop of vanilla ice cream. Garnish with the Candied Kumquats and serve immediately.

Candied Kumquats

KUMQUATS LOOK like miniature oranges. They look wonderful in arrangements of flowers and fruit, but it would be a shame to miss their fragrant aroma and intriguing texture: you can eat fresh kumquats whole, skin and all. They are seasonal items, so when you see them, grab a few containers and make these candied kumquats to enjoy for weeks to come.

MAKES 1¼ CUPS

Water, as needed

1¼ cups halved and seeded kumquats

2¼ cups granulated sugar

⅓ cup corn syrup

1. Bring a large pot of water to a boil and add the kumquats. Boil for 1 minute, then drain. Repeat twice more, using fresh water each time. Set aside.

2. Combine 1½ cups water, the sugar, and corn syrup in a saucepan and bring to a bare simmer. Add the blanched kumquats and let poach until all traces of bitterness are gone and the kumquat peel is very soft, about 1 hour and 45 minutes. (There should be only very slight action on the surface of the poaching liquid with few if any bubbles breaking the surface. Some steam should billow from the surface.)

3. Remove the pan from the heat and let the kumquats cool to room temperature in the cooking syrup. Store the kumquats in the syrup in covered containers in the refrigerator for up to 4 weeks.

GRILLED PAPAYA AND MANGO SKEWERS

with Lime Sorbet

I T IS extremely important to use ripe fruit for this. The lime sorbet is fairly tart and it needs the sweetness of the ripe fruit for balance. There is just enough sorbet to coat the fruit in a little tart syrup when it melts for a nice flavor contrast.

MAKES 8 SERVINGS

8 bamboo skewers

1 large papaya, cut into 1-inch cubes

4 medium mangoes, cut into 1-inch cubes

Key Lime Sorbet (recipe follows)

1. Soak the skewers in cool water for 30 minutes.

2. Preheat a gas grill to medium-high. If you are using a charcoal grill, build a fire and let it burn down until the coals are glowing red with a light coating of white ash. Spread the coals in an even bed. Clean the cooking grate.

3. Thread 6 pieces of each fruit onto each skewer.

4. Grill the fruit skewers over direct heat, turning as necessary, until the fruit is tender and well marked, about 5 to 6 minutes.

5. Serve the fruit skewers with the Key Lime Sorbet.

Key Lime Sorbet

K EY LIMES are very tiny and squeezing enough to make 2 cups can be time-consuming. If you prefer, substi-tute either 5 or 6 Persian limes (which have more juice) or use purchased Key lime juice.

MAKES 4 CUPS

2 cups granulated sugar

2½ cups water

3 tbsp corn syrup

2 cups Key lime juice

1. Combine the sugar, 1 cup of the water, and the corn syrup in a saucepan and bring to a boil over high heat, stirring occasionally. As soon as the sugar has melted and the boil has been reached, remove the pan from the heat and let cool to room temperature.

2. Add the lime juice and the remaining 1½ cups water, and stir until evenly blended. Transfer to a container, cover, and chill thoroughly in the refrigerator for at least 3 and up to 24 hours.

3. Freeze in an ice cream machine according to the manufacturer's instructions. Pack into storage containers and freeze for at least 2 and up to 24 hours before serving.

GRILLED BISCUIT OMELETS

with Wild Strawberries

WHEN YOU can't find wild strawberries out in the fields, you can certainly use whatever berries you can find, alone or in combination. Try other fruits as a topping as well, including peaches, pears, or bananas. Or, try the Grilled Fruit Salsa on page 195. The biscuit omelet is baked in the oven before it goes on the grill.

MAKES 8 SERVINGS

⅓ cup granulated sugar

2 large egg yolks

3 large eggs

⅔ cup cake flour, sifted

1 cup Chantilly cream (see note opposite)

4 cups wild strawberries (or other seasonal berries),
    hulled and quartered

1. Preheat oven to 450°F. Trace eight 5-inch circles on sheets of parchment paper and line baking sheets with the paper.

2. Combine the sugar, egg yolks, and eggs in a double boiler over barely simmering water and heat, whisking constantly, until frothy and warm (95°F to 100°F on an instant-read thermometer). Transfer the mixture to a large bowl.

3. Beat the mixture with a whisk or electric mixer on high speed until cool, about 10 minutes. Gently fold in the flour.

4. Transfer the mixture to a pastry bag fitted with a ⅜-inch-wide tip. Pipe the mixture in a spiral onto the parchment paper, completely filling each circle.

5. Bake the biscuit omelets until the center of an omelet springs back when gently pressed, about 6 minutes.

6. Slide the omelets, still on the parchment, onto a cold table or counter. Immediately cover with a clean cloth and let cool slightly.

7. Preheat a gas grill to high. If you are using a charcoal grill, build a fire and let it burn down until the coals are glowing red with a light coating of white ash. Spread the coals in an even bed. Clean the cooking grate.

8. Grill the biscuit omelets over direct heat until well marked on each side but still pliable, about 1 minute per side.

9. Serve the biscuit omelets warm with the Chantilly cream and berries.

Chantilly Cream

Chantilly cream gets it name from the region of France where it was famously served to King Louis XIV. To make a chantilly cream, whip well-chilled heavy cream until it thickens and add a bit of sugar (superfine or powdered sugar dissolves most easily). Continue to whip the cream until it is thick enough to spoon or pipe onto your dessert.

If you can find cream that is not stabilized and hasn't been ultra-pasteurized, your reward is a slightly stiffer, denser, richer cream.

S'MORES ARE a classic campfire dessert. Although they are traditionally made by toasting the marshmallows on a stick over an open fire, you can use your grill. Everyone has their own technique—and preferences—about toasting marshmallows, so let everyone (except small children) toast their own. For a deep golden brown and fewer flames, turn the marshmallow slowly over the flame or glowing coals, and if it starts to cook too quickly in certain spots, move the marshmallow a little farther away from the flame.

MAKES 8 SERVINGS

Eight 1-oz pieces dark, semisweet, or milk chocolate

16 Graham Cracker Cookies (recipe follows)

8 Cinnamon Marshmallows (recipe follows)

1. If you don't have a campfire burning, preheat a gas grill to high. If you are using a charcoal grill, build a fire and let it burn down until the coals are glowing red with a light coating of white ash.

2. Place 1 piece of chocolate on each of 8 graham cracker cookies.

3. Place the marshmallows on metal skewers and hold the skewers over the grill until gooey or to the desired doneness.

4. Top each chocolate-covered graham cracker with a marshmallow, then top each with one of the remaining graham cracker cookies. Serve immediately.

Cinnamon Marshmallows

MAKING YOUR own marshmallows is a fascinating process. These treats are softer and more flavorful than the kind you buy at the store, plus you can customize them by adding your own favorite flavor, like the powdered cinnamon we've used here, or by cutting them into a variety of shapes. The number of marshmallows you get from this recipe will vary, depending upon how you choose to cut them out. Regardless of the shape and size you like, remember that any extras can be packed up and stored in the freezer to enjoy another day. They thaw in just a few minutes at room temperature.

Vegetable oil, as needed

2 tbsp powdered gelatin

1 cup cold water

1½ cups granulated sugar

½ cup honey

½ cup corn syrup

1½ tsp vanilla extract

1½ tsp ground cinnamon

¼ cup cornstarch

1. Line a jelly-roll pan with parchment paper and lightly grease the parchment paper with the oil. Cut a second piece of parchment paper of the same size, oil it lightly, and set aside.

2. Sprinkle the gelatin over ½ cup of the cold water and briefly stir to completely moisten it and break up any clumps. Let the gelatin sit in the cold water until it swells and softens, 10 to 15 minutes.

3. Combine the sugar, honey, and corn syrup with the remaining ½ cup of water in a heavy-bottomed saucepan and stir to moisten the sugar. Cook over high heat, stirring constantly, until the mixture comes to a boil. Immediately stop stirring and skim the surface to remove any scum that has risen to the top. Continue to cook over high heat, occasionally brushing down the side of the pan using a pastry brush and water, until the mixture registers 242°F on a candy thermometer.

4. Remove the mixture from the heat and let cool to approximately 210°F.

5. Place the gelatin in a heatproof bowl over a pan of simmering water. Stir constantly until the mixture is clear and liquid. Mix the vanilla into the dissolved gelatin.

6. Mix the gelatin into the cooked sugar mixture and transfer to a mixing bowl. Stir in the cinnamon. Whip the mixture with an electric mixer on high speed until medium peaks form, about 8 to 10 minutes.

7. Spread the mixture in the lined pan. Top the mixture with the prepared parchment paper and use a rolling pin to spread the mixture into an even slab. Place in the freezer for at least 8 and up to 24 hours before taking the slab out of the pan.

8. Gently peel off the paper from 1 side. Lightly dust the marshmallow slab with some of the cornstarch. Flip the slab over and gently peel off the parchment paper. Dust the second side of the marshmallow slab lightly with more of the cornstarch.

9. Use a 2½-inch biscuit cutter, dipped into the cornstarch, to cut rounds, or simply cut into pieces with a sharp knife. If the cutter or knife begins to stick, dip it in additional cornstarch or dust the marshmallows lightly with a little more cornstarch.

10. Serve the marshmallows now, or store in an airtight covered container in the freezer for up to 4 months.

Graham Cracker Cookies

GRAHAM CRACKERS were actually introduced in the nineteenth century as a health food, by a minister and nutritional advocate named Sylvester Graham. Crumbs from these honey-sweetened, whole-wheat crackers are used as the basis for this delicious cookie.

MAKES 16 COOKIES

1 cup softened butter

½ cup granulated sugar

1 large egg, lightly beaten

¾ tsp vanilla extract

2½ cups cake flour

½ cup graham cracker crumbs

1. Cream together the butter and sugar by hand or with an electric mixer on medium speed, scraping down the bowl periodically, until smooth and light in color, about 5 minutes.

3. Mix in the egg and vanilla, scraping down the bowl and blending until smooth.

4. Add the flour and graham cracker crumbs all at once, mixing on low speed until just blended.

5. Turn the dough onto a floured work surface. Shape it into a flat disk, wrap tightly, and refrigerate for at least 1 hour.

6. Preheat oven to 350°F. Grease a baking sheet or line with parchment paper.

7. Roll the dough to ⅛-inch thickness. Cut sixteen 3-inch squares or rounds out of the dough, and place them on the prepared baking sheet. (Gather up the scraps and re-roll the dough as necessary.) Chill the dough in the refrigerator for 10 minutes before baking.

8. Bake the graham cracker cookies until golden brown, about 12 to 15 minutes. Let the cookies cool to room temperature on a wire rack.

9. Serve the graham cracker cookies now, or store in an airtight container at room temperature for up to 5 days.

GRILLED POUND CAKE

with Coffee Ganache

ANY GOOD-QUALITY pound cake will work in this recipe, but the cake recipe we give below makes a dense cake that slices neatly and stands up perfectly to the grill. Adding the ganache and either whipped cream or ice cream provides the perfect amount of flavor and moisture for an outstanding dessert from the grill.

MAKES 8 SERVINGS

1 Pound Cake, cut into 1-inch-thick slices (recipe follows)

1 cup Coffee Ganache (recipe follows)

1 cup whipped cream or French Vanilla Ice Cream (page 202)

1 cup coarse-chopped toasted hazelnuts

1. Preheat a gas grill to medium-high. If you are using a charcoal grill, build a fire and let it burn down until the coals are glowing red with a light coating of white ash. Spread the coals in an even bed. Clean the cooking grate.

2. Grill the Pound Cake slices until well marked on both sides of each slice and the cake is warmed throughout, about 3 to 4 minutes on each side.

3. Serve the grilled cake topped with the Coffee Ganache, whipped cream or ice cream, and toasted hazelnuts.

LEFT TO RIGHT Cream the butter and sugar together until the mixture is light and fluffy. The mixture should be loose but not broken after the eggs are added; if the mixture looks broken, mix in a little flour to bring it back together. Spoon the batter into the pans and tap them slightly to release any air bubbles that may be trapped inside.

Pound Cake

IF YOU are making your pound cake in a 4½- or 5-quart mixer, this quantity of batter fits in the bowl easily, so you may as well make two cakes! Then you can freeze one to have on hand for later.

MAKES 2 CAKES

4½ cups cake flour

3½ tsp baking powder

¾ tsp salt

1½ cups softened butter

1¾ cups granulated sugar

12 eggs, lightly beaten

1. Preheat oven to 350°F. Prepare two 8-inch loaf pans by spraying them lightly with cooking spray or lining them with parchment paper.

2. Sift the flour, baking powder, and salt together. Set aside.

3. Cream together the butter and sugar by hand or using the paddle attachment of an electric mixer until very smooth and light, about 3 minutes. Add the eggs in 4 separate additions, scraping down the bowl between each addition and mixing until very smooth.

4. Stir the flour mixture into the creamed butter mixture by hand or on low speed until the batter is evenly blended. Do not overmix.

5. Fill the prepared loaf pans ⅔ full (or measure out 2 pounds of batter into each prepared loaf pan for the most even distribution).

6. Bake until a skewer inserted near the center of a cake comes out clean, about 1 hour.

7. Let the cakes cool in the pans for a few minutes, then transfer to wire racks to cool completely.

8. Cut the cake into slices and serve, or wrap and store whole cakes in the freezer for up to 1 month.

Coffee Ganache

YOU CAN cut this recipe in half if you prefer, but ganache keeps well in the refrigerator, so we've made a big batch so you can keep this sauce on hand to use whenever you like, even if you don't have the grill on.

MAKES 3 CUPS

2 tbsp powdered instant espresso

¼ cup boiling water

1½ cups heavy cream

2 tbsp light corn syrup

2⅔ cups finely chopped dark chocolate

1. Stir together the instant espresso and boiling water until smooth. Set aside.

2. Combine the cream and the corn syrup in a heavy saucepan and bring to a boil over medium heat. Remove the pan from the heat and stir in the espresso. Pour the mixture over the chocolate and let sit, covered, for 2 to 3 minutes. Stir until the chocolate has completely melted and the sauce is very smooth.

3. Keep warm until ready to use, or let cool to room temperature and store in a container with a tight-fitting lid in the refrigerator for up to 2 weeks. Reheat chilled sauce over very low heat on the stovetop or in the microwave until warm enough to pour easily.

GRILLED ANGEL FOOD CAKE

with Fresh Berries

ANGEL FOOD cake, though light and delicate to the bite, has enough resilience to go on the grill. The sugar in the cake takes on a deep caramel taste for an intriguing take on strawberry shortcake. Try flavoring the Chantilly cream with a liqueur or other flavor to add another dimension of flavor to this dish.

MAKES 12 SERVINGS

¾ cup cake flour

1 cup granulated sugar

Pinch salt

6 egg whites

1 tsp vanilla extract

Pinch cream of tartar

2 cups Chantilly cream (see page 213)

4 cups strawberries, hulled and halved

1. Preheat oven to 350°F.

2. Sift together the flour, ½ cup of the sugar, and the salt. Set aside.

3. Combine the egg whites, vanilla, and cream of tartar in a large bowl and whip with a whisk or beat on medium speed using the whip attachment of an electric mixer until frothy. Gradually add the remaining ½ cup sugar and beat to medium-stiff peaks.

4. Gently fold the sifted dry ingredients into the beaten egg whites just until evenly blended. Immediately pour the batter into an ungreased tube cake pan.

5. Bake until the cake springs back when lightly touched, 35 to 40 minutes. Allow the cake to completely cool upside down on a cooling rack before removing it from the pan.

6. Preheat a gas grill to medium-high. If you are using a charcoal grill, build a fire and let it burn down until the coals are glowing red with a light coating of white ash. Spread the coals in an even bed. Clean the cooking grate.

7. Cut the cake into 12 wedges. Grill the wedges until well marked on both sides and warmed through, about 3 to 4 minutes on each side.

8. Serve the grilled cake topped with the Chantilly cream and strawberries.

Baking Angel Food Cake

Angel food cake is baked in an ungreased pan so that the batter can cling to the sides as the cake bakes. Then, to protect the fragile structure of the cake just as it comes from the oven, turn the pan upside down and set it on top of a wine bottle. Let it cool completely before you try to get the cake out of the pan.

To release the cake from the pan, run a thin blade around the edges of the pan. Work carefully to avoid cutting into the cake.

INDEX

Weight Measures Conversion

U.S. and Metric. Values have been rounded.

¼ ounce	8 grams
½ ounce	15 grams
1 ounce	30 grams
4 ounces	115 grams
8 ounces (½ pound)	225 grams
16 ounces (1 pound)	450 grams
32 ounces (2 pounds)	900 grams
40 ounces (2¼ pounds)	1 kilogram

Volume Measures Conversion

U.S. and Metric. Values have been rounded.

1 teaspoon	5 milliliters
1 tablespoon	15 milliliters
1 fluid ounce (2 tablespoons)	30 milliliters
2 fluid ounces (¼ cup)	60 milliliters
8 fluid ounces (1 cup)	240 milliliters
16 fluid ounces (1 pint)	480 milliliters
32 fluid ounces (1 quart)	950 milliliters
128 fluid ounces (1 gallon)	3.75 liters

Temperature Conversion

Degrees Farenheit and Celcius.
Values have been rounded.

32°F	0°C
40°F	4°C
140°F	60°C
150°F	65°C
160°F	70°C
170°F	75°C
212°F	100°C
275°F	135°C
300°F	150°C
325°F	165°C
350°F	175°C
375°F	190°C
400°F	205°C
425°F	220°C
450°F	230°C
475°F	245°C
500°F	260°C

A NOTE ON THE TYPE

This book was set in the OpenType version of Utopia,
a typeface designed by Robert Slimbach for the Adobe Corporation in 1989.
The highly contrasting stroke of Utopia's letterforms, inspired by 18th-century
transitional typefaces like Baskerville and Walbaum, is combined with more
contemporary character shapes and energetic calligraphic details to
create a unique, modern interpretation of those types.

Art direction, design, and composition by Kevin Hanek
Printed in Singapore by Imago Worldwide Printing